THE REAL READER'S Q

Slightly Foxed

'Attics with Attitude'

NO.36   WINTER 2012

Editors Gail Pirkis and Hazel Wood
Marketing and publicity Stephanie Allen and Jennie Paterson
Subscriptions Alarys Gibson and Anna Kirk

Cover illustration: Angela Harding, 'Bringing Back the Tree'
Angela Harding is a painter and printmaker based in Wing, Rutland. She derives her inspiration
from the flora and fauna of the British countryside and her work is executed in lino and vinyl,
combined with paper-cut stencil and water-based silkscreen printing. She exhibits nationally and
her illustrations have been published in magazines and as greeting cards. She is currently
illustrating a monthly column for *Gardens Illustrated*. For more about her work, see
www.angelaharding.co.uk.

Design by Octavius Murray, layout by Andrew Evans, colophon and tailpiece by David Eccles

© The contributors 2012

We have moved to

53 Hoxton Square, London NI 6PB
tel 020 7033 0258
www.foxedquarterly.com

Slightly Foxed is published quarterly in early March, June, September and December
Annual subscription rates (4 issues)
UK £36; Europe £44; Rest of the World £48
Concessions are available for those aged 26 or under: please call the office
Single copies of this issue can be bought for £9 (UK), £11 (Europe) or £12 (Rest of the World)
Back issues are also available

ISBN 978-1-906562-43-4
Printed and bound by Smith Settle, Yeadon, West Yorkshire

Contents

Contents

Miriam Macgregor, 'Winter Garden'

From the Editors

It seems, as they say, only yesterday that we were telling you *Slightly Foxed* would be moving – in fact it was in 2004 that we moved from our original 'office' round the kitchen table of Gail's home in Canonbury to the family's new home in Clerkenwell. For eight years we roosted gratefully at Dickinson Court, gradually expanding, like the proverbial cuckoo, until we'd virtually taken over; turning the spare room into a post room, filling every available alcove with back issues and filing trays, and the hall with bicycles and parcels of books.

So last month it was time to move again – to a proper grown-up office just down the road, in Hoxton Square, which is thought to be one of the oldest squares in London. For those of you not familiar with the area, it's a part of London that has fairly recently had a re-birth and is now home to little restaurants and cutting-edge art galleries like White Cube. But it still retains its original East London feel, and when we say 'office' we're not talking about lifts and switchboards and water-coolers. Our new home (53 Hoxton Square, London N1 6PB) is in a building which was once a warehouse, and when we've properly settled in we'll still be wrapping up books and sending out issues, sitting around the same kitchen table to chew things over, and answering the phone ourselves.

It's an exciting moment, but moving office did bring on a wave of nostalgia as we remembered the early years, the fun we had setting *Slightly Foxed* up, the way our early subscribers – many of you, gratifyingly, still with us – rallied round, putting the word about and supporting us with letters and phone calls, despite some rather gloomy predictions at the time. We may be a bit bigger now, but we're glad to say that we still have fun, we still love *Slightly Foxed* and everything that goes with it, especially the contact we have with our readers, who are as interested and supportive as ever they were. A big thank-you to you all.

But hankies away now, and on to the present with the latest of the Slightly Foxed Editions, a delightful dual memoir by the writer and illustrator Denis Constanduros (see p. 12). First published in 1948, *My Grandfather*, as its title indicates, is an affectionate and delicately humorous portrait of the author's maternal grandfather and his household in the early years of the last century. *Father, Dear Father* – once read to much acclaim on Radio 4 but published now for the first time – is an irresistibly funny, but ultimately poignant account of Denis's extraordinary childhood and of the other important figure in his life, his father. A little gem of a book, and highly recommended both as a cheering winter read and a delightful Christmas present.

This time last year we ran a very successful Young Writers' Competition, and this year we've decided it's time to give our older readers a chance. So if you're 60 or over and have a favourite book you'd like to write about why not enter? We're looking for a piece of not more than 1,500 words, written in characteristic *SF* style – which is to say a piece that reflects your own experience of the book and why you have chosen it, and makes other people want to read it too. The winner will receive £250 and the piece will be published in *Slightly Foxed*, while the runner-up will appear on our website. Entries should reach us by 28 February. For more information see our website www.foxedquarterly.com or phone us at the office.

And finally, just to keep the grey cells in good order, we've got another of our literary crosswords for you – it's on the back of the leaflet slipped into this issue. Entries should reach us no later than 14 January and the first correct one to be drawn out of a hat will receive a free annual subscription.

GAIL PIRKIS

HAZEL WOOD

Attics with Attitude

ELISABETH RUSSELL TAYLOR

I am sometimes asked which writers have changed my life. Next time I shall not answer 'Proust' but 'Rachel Khoo'. For five years, since the death of my husband, I had all but given up cooking and eating, all but forgotten what I had valued before my personal doomsday. Rachel Khoo has re-engaged my taste-buds and my enthusiasm. I may even convert my fantasy dinner parties into real ones. I am already making lists.

In 1951, I exchanged a comfortable flat in London for an uncomfortable attic in Paris. I was young, I was making a statement in the face of bourgeois values – those of money, privilege and entitlement: I was choosing slender means. As a result, every aspect of my new life revealed to me a different version of myself from the one imposed by my background.

The word 'attic' is loaded with ambiguity. One has only to look to literature, where it can stand variously for the romantic and the corrupt – for a mouse-infested eyrie with creaking floorboards, filled with the dust and dirt of centuries, but also for a haven of warmth, privacy and creativity. When Fanny Price is consigned to bed in the attic at Mansfield Park by the horrid Mrs Norris, it is to degrade her; yet when the Brontë children needed somewhere private to compose their stories, they chose the attic. Charlotte Brontë's Mr Rochester keeps his mad wife Bertha prisoner in the attic; but when Jo March is fighting against the life of marriage and domesticity proposed for

Rachel Khoo, *The Little Paris Kitchen* (2012)
Michael Joseph · Hb · 288pp · £20 · ISBN 9780718158118

her in *Little Women*, it is to the attic that she escapes.

On a daily basis, life in an attic is challenging: the roof can leak, delivery men refuse the stairs like horses refusing a jump, and if the entry-phone is out of order and one is ill, there is nothing for it but to hurl the key from the window into the road and risk it disappearing down a drain – but if one's leg is in plaster and one is on crutches, how can one manage the stairs?

My recent reflections on attic life were prompted by an ineluctable force which drove me to buy *The Little Paris Kitchen* (2012) by Rachel Khoo, a young Englishwoman who decamped to France to learn to cook. I tend not to buy cookery books nowadays, I borrow them from the library instead. But Rachel Khoo, producing exemplary French cuisine in a confined space, struck a chord at the back of my mind which seemed to re-awaken in me the acknowledgement that difficulty in the creation of anything worth striving for is important.

From a tiny kitchen with standing space for one, Rachel Khoo simplifies classic French cooking without losing anything of its reliance on first-class ingredients and home-made stocks, sauces and *pâtisserie*. She pursues her passion in order to share it with friends and strangers alike. She can only seat two at a time in her miniscule dining area but she puts into what she serves the same passion as she would for a gathering of gourmets. She has built up relationships with independent suppliers; she has made her daily round in the market, at the *pâtisserie* and *boucherie*, a way of life – the French way.

She is Cordon Bleu-trained and understands the chemistry of cookery, but she chooses to adopt a casual style to encourage readers to follow her recipes; her *quenelles de volailles* are prepared in a blender in a single minute and her *sabayon aux Saint-Jacques* in ten. She understands the place of food in French life and sees no reason why it should not find similar status in the English-speaking world. Eating is for her a social activity; I notice that her balcony has no planting: she needs every square centimetre free for her guests to stand, one hand round an apéritif, an arm around a friend.

Markets in London are not as enticing as those in Paris. It would seem that neither the beauty of our countryside, nor that of other countries where produce is grown, affects those who display it in London. And there are few independent cheese shops, butchers and fishmongers. We have to make do with supermarkets, which for me removes one of the principal delights in the preparation of food. Chicken carcasses for stock are available, but only three miles north of my attic, as is an excellent fishmonger; properly stored cheeses, with knowledgeable assistants to advise, are cut off by the

Tom Fairs

Congestion Charge zone; exceptionally the butcher is at hand. In Paris, in my area of Fontenay-sous-Bois, the locals slipped out in their nightwear for their breakfast baguette and shopped every morning in the local market.

I had been used to years of food rationing when I settled in Paris. If you lived in a town in England (it was different in the country), you were lucky not to go hungry, and food was regarded merely as fuel. I have no memory of markets. Anyhow, we had to 'register' with a particular shop to which we had to give our ration card. There was guilt about striving to find anything beyond our exiguous rations, for only 'spivs' bought and sold on the black market. At the same time, in Paris, the most despised vegetable was being attractively displayed and cooked with loving care; food was affordable and plentiful, meals were lingered over, ingredients discussed and respected. Everyone bought bread twice a day and ground their coffee in the home, for it was expected that both would be fresh at every sitting. No outing was complete without the consumption of some small pastry or drink, for enjoyment was not a charge against morality. I wanted all that for myself, as a foundation stone of my new life.

My Paris attic had a cold-water tap, two gas rings but no fridge, larder, hand-mixer or blender. There was no money to spend on buying equipment or installing improvements. I learned to cook by placing one saucepan on top of another to steam vegetables and fish, and to 'roast' by plunging meat into vegetable oil in a deep saucepan. I adopted the French habit of buying food daily, of using herbs and spices, making stock and sauces, and drinking rough wine. I discovered that salad was not a lettuce leaf and a couple of slices of beetroot and cucumber, that half a grapefruit with a cherry at its centre was not a starter, and that noodles and rice can be transformed by a herb butter or a home-made sauce. This was four years before Elizabeth David started to educate us in paperback.

In 1962, I found myself in an attic in London without gas and electricity, but this time I was in a position to have services installed. My husband encouraged me to respect the craft of cookery with the best tools I could afford: stainless steel, ceramic and cast-iron, and knives for the different purposes for which they had been forged. I was in thrall to attic life: no basement, even with access to a garden, could have enticed me from my eyrie. My kitchen, where the slope of the roof reduced leg room to a mere 6 by 4 foot 6, must provide for a dining-table which seated eight. I papered the walls in a red and orange French design in homage to Vuillard, my favourite painter of the domestic scene. I have always regretted that my attic was not in Paris.

However, whether in London or Paris, attics share disadvantages: mine has 63 steps to ascend from street level. Unlike some Northern European cities, neither London nor Paris has made provision for pulleys. Eccentric residents have been known to tie a basket to a very long rope and let their cat out once or twice a day, but otherwise everything has to be carted by hand up and down the stairs. But attics share advantages, too, and my view over London is one such. In winter, as I lie in bed, St Paul's crouches between my feet; in summer a huge ash, in florid leaf, protects my view from architecturally uninspired flats usurping the space once filled by beautiful old stables.

I have planted a cottage garden on a balcony (10 by 6 feet) leading from my bedroom, and another on a wide ledge outside the living-room window facing south-west. Both surfaces rest below the highest branches of the tree, as if suspended in air. And being at different heights, the jasmine, the roses, the everlasting sweet peas and akebia climb and tumble between the two, over the roof, around the pipes and the window frames. There is space for a table and two chairs and when I am neither reading there nor working at my plants, song birds, woodpeckers, jays and parakeets visit to feed from the nut cage.

Rachel Khoo's *The Little Paris Kitchen* encourages me to make of a fantasy a reality again, to bring into my eighties what enchanted me when I was in my twenties.

When she is not cooking for friends in her attic eyrie, ELISABETH RUSSELL TAYLOR is feeding the birds. Her novels are available as Virago Modern Classics.

Sherry Wine and Roses

HAZEL WOOD

In the Devon village where I grew up, the main cultural event – in fact the *only* cultural event – was the Women's Institute Drama Competition. It was held in the summer holidays, in the town hall of our local market town, and it went on for two or three days. For a child who had never been to the theatre the whole affair was magical, and excitement in the audience was intense as local WIs competed with one another in scenes from Shakespeare and, very often it seemed, in one-act plays by someone with the strange name of Mabel Constanduros. She seemed to be as much part of the whole thing as the hard wooden chairs, the interval tea and cakes, and the bus ride home through the summer-scented lanes, and I sometimes wondered who she was – a question I never pursued but which was recently answered for me in an unexpected way.

Not long after we launched the Slightly Foxed Editions, we came across a little gem of a book, first published in 1948 and long out of print, which we decided we must reissue. *My Grandfather*, as its title indicates, is a portrait of the author's maternal grandfather, who, though surviving sturdily into the reign of George V, was to his grandson a character from the 'warm, gas-lit, stable-smelling past' of the Victorian age. With delicate and affectionate humour it brings to life not only its central character, but also the world in which he lived, and which he surveyed with genial content from the windows of his spacious home in Kensington Gore.

The book was so delightful, so pitch-perfect in every way, it made us curious to know more about its author, Denis Constanduros – the aforementioned Mabel's nephew as it turns out – and at this point we made an exciting discovery. There was, we learned, an unpublished companion volume, *Father, Dear Father*, which, like *My Grandfather*, had once been read to much acclaim on Radio 4. We decided to publish both together for the first time, and to include some of the author's previously unpublished drawings. *Father, Dear Father* fills in, in an equally diverting way, the story of Denis's childhood in the shadow of the other important male figure in his life – his father.

The two could hardly have been more different. Grandfather symbolized, in his person and his habits, everything that was convivial, straightforward and reliable. His was the very spirit of an age in which, as the author says, 'Life was simple and clear-cut. There were no complexities and half-tones.' His son-in-law Stephanos ('Steph') Constanduros, on the other hand, was flamboyant, melodramatic, full of grand ideas for solving his perpetual financial problems 'at a stroke', and inclined to take refuge from unpleasantness in ill health.

The son of a Greek political émigré, Steph had initially charmed his future father-in-law – and his future wife, who was then only 15 – with his fine voice, his singing of sentimental songs and his careless insouciance. (Once, while in full song, standing under a lighted gas jet, his hair caught fire but he continued singing 'undisturbed'. Grandfather, always susceptible to the power of music, had spontaneously clapped his hands and cried 'Bravo! Bravo!' – a gesture of approval which, as his grandson observes, he must have regretted for the rest of his life.)

In appearance Grandfather himself was 'short and round, with a face that was cherubic in its benignity'. He seemed, to his grandson, a compound of Mr Jorrocks, whom he read, admired and quoted, and – most strikingly – his great hero, Mr Pickwick. 'As he stood at the window, chumping his false teeth slightly and perhaps whistling under his breath "Oh Rest in the Lord" or a favourite air from *The Beggar's Opera*, the likeness was remarkable.'

Grandfather's household in Kensington was certainly Victorian in its size and composition. Grown-up children had flown the nest, but

 Grandmother's unmarried sisters from Croydon were regular guests – Aunt Maria, 'a stolid, black, unlovely figure' engaged in a perpetual game of Patience; and Aunt Pem, who was given to laughing immoderately 'until the veins on the side of her fragile head stood out in blue relief. She laughed immoderately, not because she was particularly amused, but because it was the only way she could show emotion.'

Below stairs were to be found old Lucy, haunted by constant thoughts of impending disaster (she it was who decided that a purple bath mat was too bright for Grandfather – she feared the sight of it, as he rose suddenly from his daily cold bath, might bring on a stroke) and fat, jolly, carefree old Ellen the cook. The household was completed by a 'young girl', Jonzen the deep-voiced Swedish parlourmaid, and Parsons the chauffeur, who drove Grandfather to Epping every Wednesday where, much to everyone's consternation, he rode to hounds with his old friend Mr Fitch.

Images summon up that distant time: Grandfather, toasting his feet cosily before the fire in Mr Fitch's farmhouse after a good day's hunting; stumping on his short legs through the hushed galleries of the Royal Academy to admire a favourite painting; resplendent in silk top hat at the Richmond Horse Show; perusing the obituary columns of '*The Times* Newspaper'; or pouring a glass of what he called 'sherry wine'.

And sounds too: the early-morning cacophony of 'trilling sopranos, thumping pianos and scraping violins' that daily reached the household from the nearby Royal College of Music; the evening tolling of the park keeper's bell and the cries of 'All out!'; the secure and comforting sound made by the closing of the house's heavy front door – *My Grandfather* is much more than a marvellous evocation of an endearing yet tough and sometimes perverse old character. Nothing dramatic happens in it, yet everything happens – it is a meditation on an age and has the texture of life itself.

Father, Dear Father, Denis's account of his own childhood, is much more like one of those comedies for which his Aunt Mabel was later to become famous. Doors (usually of down-at-heel rented houses) open and close; characters enter and exit, and, as the action speeds up, often collide dramatically. Among these, in no particular order, are Steph's brother Athanasius ('Uncle Ath'), a contrastingly Pooteresque, hardworking and solvent character who had married another of Grandfather's daughters, the not-yet-famous Aunt Mabel; 'Mac', the glamorous but sinisterly controlling air ace who, after the First World War, became the family's lodger; his wartime buddy Oscar, who was studying to become an operatic baritone; and a series of tutors employed to teach Denis and his brother – most notably Captain Wilson, who had no more interest in teaching than the boys had in learning, and who was a great practical joker and rather too fond of the bottle. The main background to this tragi-comedy – which is what the story turned into – were two hideous adjoining houses in Sutton: Melton, finally purchased for the family by Grandfather after Steph – a practising but possibly unqualified architect – ran out of money; and Belhaven, in which resided Aunt Mabel and Uncle Ath.

Steph was a keen gardener and in summer Captain Wilson, a first-class bluffer and anxious to curry favour since his position was always precarious, would stand behind Steph's deckchair secretly consulting a rose catalogue, and engage him in conversation, throwing out knowing remarks about the roses ('Caroline Testout is a lovely climber I always think, don't you sir?'), the benefits of a dressing of bone meal and the importance of 'disbudding'. Steph was in raptures. Bluffing was a tendency shared by vivacious Aunt Mabel. If the vicar called she would be overheard earnestly discussing the efficacy of prayer, though she never went to church. 'I always give my fruitcakes a good hour and a half in a slow oven' she would tell women callers, though she never went near the kitchen.

But the greatest bluffer of all was probably Steph himself. *Father, Dear Father* is a wonderful study in self-delusion. Returning in the evening from his office in the City and sinking into the nearest armchair he would make some dramatic pronouncement.

'Well,' he would say, 'how would you all like to go to South America? A chap came into my office today and said "I want to see Constanduros – the expert. I don't want to see any of the others." He's got some big scheme to build a huge hydro-electric dam in Bolivia. If it comes off it'll be something important for all of us.'

Unfortunately the reality was very different. In hock to his bookmaker, Steph had, as his son writes, 'a natural affinity' with all bankrupts. 'If he didn't seek them out they sought him. And some, who were financially normal when he befriended them, at once became bankrupt, as though simply to conform.'

This was a household in denial. Nothing was ever mended. 'The system in our house', Denis remembers, 'was that anything that was likely to bring my father face to face with the reality of our situation was to be stowed away out of sight.' Games of all kinds, in which everyone but Denis's long-suffering mother took part, became a kind of displacement activity. The house and garden rang daily to the sounds of table tennis, a strange game called Puff Billiards which was played with 'a thing like an old-fashioned motor horn', an even stranger one called Wibbly Wob, and Hoicky Hockey (played on the tennis lawn with a football and walking sticks). As relations became more strained and the financial situation grew more desperate, so the action became more and more manic, like a speeded-up film.

It couldn't last, and eventually the whole farrago collapsed in a way that was both ludicrous and poignant. Fortunately, we learned from Denis's daughters, in real life there was a happier sequel. Like Aunt

Mabel, with whom he initially collaborated, Denis built a highly successful career for himself as an illustrator and a writer for radio, stage and screen. How pleasingly paradoxical that such a chaotic and rather desperate childhood should have given rise to two such elegant and light-hearted little books.

Before becoming a journalist, HAZEL WOOD read Drama at Bristol University but she has never taken part in a drama competition, or indeed trodden the boards.

My Grandfather & *Father, Dear Father* (272 pp) are now available from *Slightly Foxed* as a single volume, in a new limited and numbered cloth-bound pocket edition of 2,000 copies, priced at £13.50 (plus p&p: UK £2.50, Europe £4.50, Rest of the World £5.50). Copies may be ordered by post (53 Hoxton Square, London NI 6PB), by phone (020 7033 0258) or via our website www.foxedquarterly.com.

Denis in later life, in the shepherd's hut where he worked

Along the Old Ways

ROBERT MACFARLANE

For many years of my life, I was fascinated by mountains and their tops: drawn upwards by what Joe Simpson nicely calls 'the inverted gravity' that peaks exert upon certain people. I climbed and mountaineered – ineptly but passionately – in ranges around the world: Snowdonia, the Lake District, the Cuillins, the Cairngorms, the Alps, the Rockies, the Tian Shan, the Himalayas. All of these expeditions, from half-day to multi-month, were centred upon summits. My companions and I would scry our maps, mark the tops we wished to reach, then plan our journeys around those high points. It did not occur to me to explore a mountain without reference to its peak.

These days I still love mountains, but I find myself just as interested in their passes and paths as in their summits; just as intrigued by the valleys and notches that have been gouged out of them by ice and by water, and the tracks that have been worn into them by the passage of animals and humans. The Cairngorm mountains of Scotland, the range I know best, are most famous for their tops: the Cairngorm itself, lonely Ben Avon with its granite tors, sharp and shapely Cairn Toul, and the grey peak of Ben Macdui, from which I have retreated on two occasions in winter, chased southwards on skis and on foot by raving boreal blizzards.

But the Cairngorms also contain one of Britain's greatest valleys, the Lairig Ghru, which divides the massif into two main groups, and which rises to a pass at 835 metres – higher than many British moun-

A. R. B. Haldane, *The Drove Roads of Scotland* (1952)
Birlinn · Pb · 266pp · £8.99 · ISBN 9781841586953

tains. The traverse of the Cairngorms by means of the Lairig Ghru is a reasonable challenge for a modern-day walker. It is bouldery, high and wild, and requires long tramps in from either end. Its entrances are guarded by sentinel peaks, in winter it is snow-scoured, and in summer the midges emerge in their millions (midges like me a great deal; I, consequently, dislike them a great deal).

Whenever I am in the Lairig Ghru, and feeling tired, or footsore, or otherwise put upon by its asperities, I think of the drovers: the men who moved livestock through Scotland in the centuries before refrigerated trucks, licensed abattoirs, the A9 and the M80 – and who were surely some of the toughest walkers in British history. The drovers, wrote Sir John Sinclair with grudging admiration in his *Analysis of the Statistical Account* (1825), were 'accustomed to scanty fare, to rude and often wet clothing, to cold and damp houses, to sleep often in the open air, to cross dangerous rivers, to march a number of miles without stopping and with but little nourishment, and to be perpetually exposed to the attacks of a stormy atmosphere'. The memory of which description is enough to put steel in the backbone and a spring in the step of any Gore-Tex-clad, Vibram-sole-wearing, manchego-and-chilli-chutney-sandwich-carrying contemporary walker such as myself.

Through the droving years, the Ghru was the main route across the Cairngorm massif, taking cattle down through Glen Lui and then on south to Braemar. Sheep coming from Skye would occasionally be driven across the pass, and its last recorded use as a drove route was in 1873. The Ghru posed problems to the drovers in terms of distance and severity of weather and terrain. Each winter brought fresh falls from the surrounding crags, and the upper reaches of the valley would become crowded with leg-breaking boulders, ill-suited to the soft hooves and long legs of cattle. So it was that late each spring, once the snow had at last begun to melt, men were sent up to the high pass to shift the boulders and open the path.

I know what I know of the drovers because of a remarkable and modest book called *The Drove Roads of Scotland* (1952) by A. R. B. Haldane, which I read first ten years or so ago, and then again in 2008, shortly before I walked across the Cairngorms from Blair Atholl to Aviemore in order to attend my grandfather's funeral. It is renowned as the bible of droving history, and more broadly as a classic of Scottish history, and it introduced me – as it has introduced so many others – to the remnant traces of a vanished culture.

'During the autumn of 1942', the book begins, 'I had occasion, in the course of certain work on which I was then engaged, to call to mind an old road which crosses the Ochils immediately behind my home near Auchterarder in Perthshire.' Well, this is a sentence which – with its subtle rhythms, its controlled discretion and its swift adventure into memory – would not feel out of place at the start of one of W. G. Sebald's paragraphs. It beckons the reader into the book as a path might beckon a walker's feet. The beckoning continues:

> For a mile or two back into the hills, the road serves as an access to upland farms, but at the sheep farm of Coulshill it loses this character, and from that point to its junction with the main road through Glendevon, it is now little more than a lonely grass-grown track crossing the hills. Little used as it now is, the grassy road retains the clear marks of extensive use by the traffic of former days, and it occurred to me that it would be of interest to try to trace something of its history.

Haldane started to dig back into the archive, to interview men and women in many parts of Scotland, and also to walk the landscape – following the shadows of the old drove roads where they could still be glimpsed in text, in memory and in the earth. He researched his subject for eight years before he began to write about it, gradually piecing together the story of the drove roads of Scotland.

What Haldane discovered was that there are few Highland glens that were not used at one point as a route for the drovers, whose work was a major feature of Highland and Island life between the Act of

Union in 1707 and the trade's decline in the second quarter of the nineteenth century. Illegal droving, mostly by reavers (cattle thieves) had dated back to the sixteenth century, but it was the agricultural revolution and the pacifying of the Highlands by General Wade after the 1715 rebellion that greatly extended the licensed droving industry. Cattle were the chief form of movable wealth in the Highlands, and they had to be brought from their grazing grounds down to the markets in the Lowlands and the Borders. A network of tracks, paths and practices came into existence to make this movement possible, and

Kathleen Lindsley, 'Cooling off – Dunvegan'

this network was what Haldane reconstructed (the 1971 hardback edition I own contains a fine fold-out map on which the routes and gathering areas are inked in red and black lines).

Reading Haldane has transformed the way I understand the Highlands. He taught me how to follow on foot the routes of the drove roads, and to look for the patches of open ground that would have been the 'stances' of the drovers: the resting-places, close to water and on level ground, where the men could sleep and the livestock could graze. And he introduced me to the drovers themselves: these hard men, the long-distance lorry-drivers of their day, accustomed to the boredoms and rigours of their journeys, and equipped with internalized sat-navs of astonishing accuracy. They navigated not from maps but from memories, stories and gossip. Walter Scott in his *The Two Drovers* described them as being 'required to know perfectly the drove roads which lie over the wildest tracts of the country, and to avoid as much as possible the highways which distress the feet of the bullocks, and the turnpikes which annoy the spirit of the drover'.

What a sight a great drove must have been! Up to three hundred beasts and half a dozen drovers, some on foot and some on ponies, with their dogs, moving through country unmarked by tracks other than their own. The men on foot carrying 'cromachs' (sticks used to belt and berate the swaying stirks as well as for walking). Ten miles covered in a day, perhaps twelve: no more or the beasts would lose condition and value. There would be grazing stops at midday, and river crossings where necessary – the cattle pushed into the water, the drovers swimming alongside them and crying loudly to keep them moving. The drovers had no interest in summits, of course; only in passes, glens and river valleys.

The traffic of the livestock was often referred to in contemporary descriptions as consisting of 'streams' of beasts, and indeed the characteristic marks of a drove road are similar to those left by the passage of a stream – alternately flowing in broad shallows or narrow deeps and rapids. The drovers emptied the Highlands and Islands of their livestock each year, draining them down towards 'trysts' (cattle fairs) at Stirling and Falkirk, with some of the cattle continuing even down to London – a south-flowing torrent of beasts, of beef, of capital.

Haldane's book – though wary of nostalgia and rigorous in its historiography – has a tinge of elegy to it, to which I am wholly susceptible. In his account the drovers, though resilient in the face of hardship, were by no means impervious to beauty. They relished, some of them at least, a love of movement and adventure. And they left behind them the traces of a fascinating age:

The brown sails of the cattle boats have gone from the Minch. On slipways and jetties from Skye to Kintyre, thrift grows undisturbed in the crannies of stones once smooth and polished with the tread of hooves. Lonely saltings where the Uist droves once grazed, and throughout the Highlands in hill pass and moorland, as in the minds of men, the passing years increasingly dim and obscure the mark and the memory of the men and beasts that once travelled the drove roads of Scotland.

ROBERT MACFARLANE is the author of *Mountains of the Mind* (2003), *The Wild Places* (2007) and most recently *The Old Ways: A Journey on Foot* (2012). Despite being a mountain-lover, he lives in Cambridge.

Perfick Wevver

SUE GEE

It is a glorious afternoon in May. In the cab of his gentian-blue truck, with six children licking enormous ice creams in the back, skinny little Pop Larkin, crammed next to enormous Ma, starts the engine and drives along Kentish lanes lined with apple orchards and strawberry fields. As he approaches home he is, as so often, in a state of complete contentment.

The dusty yard in which he pulls up is a happy muddle of nettles, scrap iron and poultry. There are also two horses, belonging to Mariette, his eldest daughter and his darling, an exquisitely slender 17-year-old in jodhpurs and lemon shirt, 'black-haired, soft-eyed, olive-skinned' – and, he has just learned from Ma, expecting a baby. It is she who draws Pop's attention to a man standing by the horse-box, watching them.

The Inland Revenue has come to call. Its pale young representative produces from his briefcase a buff form.

Things are about to change – but not, it transpires, for Pop. It is pale, nervous, desk-bound Mr Charlton – Cedric, but no one can bring themselves to call him that – whose old life now begins to unravel, as the form and all attendant questions are breezily waved aside. Already entranced by the sight of Mariette, he is invited into the kitchen. A gorgeous tea is set before him. Children crowd round, geese gobble scraps beneath the table, Ma, 'huge as a buffalo', pre-

H. E. Bates, *The Darling Buds of May* (1958)
Penguin · Pb · 144pp · £8.99 · ISBN 9780141029672
The Vanished World (1969) is out of print.

sides, washing everything down with Guinness. The room is lit by the 'pallid, unreal glow' of the television. Briefly, it is switched off.

In the half-darkness that now smothered the room, Mr Charlton felt something smooth, sinuous and slender brush against his right calf. For one shimmering, unnerving moment he sat convinced that it was Mariette's leg entwining itself about his own.

He looks down, sees a goose eating half-cold chips, and struggles to return to the question of income.

'Six kids to feed and clothe,' Pop said. 'This place to run. Fodder to buy. Wheat as dear as gold-dust . . . Vet's fees. Fowl pest. Foot-and-mouth. Swine fever. Income, old man? *Income?* I should like some, old man.'

And then, since the chips and fresh pineapple are too much for Mr Charlton's delicate stomach, Mariette is making soft-boiled eggs, laid on a plate 'embroidered with the thinnest white bread-and-butter', and Pop is speaking of the nearby woods where the bluebells are 'fick as carpets, ficker in fact', and before very long Mr Charlton finds himself invited first to Sunday lunch and then on a woodland walk with Mariette, now changed into a delicious summer frock.

On the path, lit by the broken gold of evening sunlight, he stands listening to an outburst of passionate birdsong. Mariette turns to him, takes his face in her hands. 'A moment later, he saw her lips upraised.'

Within days, the buff form bites the dust, and the chaps in the office and the 'vast and frightful' papers on his desk are forgotten. Pale Mr Charlton takes sick leave, grows brown and fit, and succumbs to paradise.

* * *

Herbert Ernest Bates was born in 1905, in Northamptonshire, the son of a cobbler, and his schooldays were spent in a brick-terraced industrial town dominated by factories where he dreaded he would one day have to work. But his Methodist childhood was lit up by visits to his grandfather's farm, and the early chapters of his memoir *The Vanished World* (1969) are full of his love of the Midlands countryside.

Every morning was golden; even the First World War had not begun. The hedgerows of spring were clothed with the cream of May-blossom; those of June and July with pink and white dogroses, meadow-sweet and willow-herb . . . Sticklebacks were in the brook, cuckoos called from the elms, yellowhammers swooned away long summer afternoons in lanes shimmering with heat . . .

The Darling Buds of May, published in 1958, is suffused with just such lyrical descriptions, and in his reconnection with a longed-for vanished world Bates produced a minor classic. Of all his novels, and he published at least twenty, with many more short-story collections, this – dramatized on ITV in the early Nineties – is the work which everyone knows and loves.

Like Mole in *The Wind in the Willows*, Mr Charlton is a fellow whose horizons need broadening, and, as with Mole, they are well and truly broadened. Like Toad, with whom he shares a love of the good life and a disdain for practicalities, Pop is a one-off. And Larkin-land is quintessential English countryside at its loveliest. Beneath a flax-blue sky, brimming hedgerows run alongside fields full of rising oats and barley, the hot summery distances are full of calling cuckoos, the woods of nightingales, the night sky of 'young unquenchable summer stars'.

Into this setting happiness pours like honey: through Ma, 'shaking like a jelly' every time she laughs, which is often; through Pop, never without a lethal cocktail, or a wad of notes, never without a scheme or a purchase – a yellow Rolls-Royce, complete with speaking tube, appears in the junk yard over this weekend; through the falling in love of Mr Charlton and Mariette (who turns out not to be pregnant after all, though someone else is) and in the endless, lavish meals to which the less fortunate inhabitants of the village are liberally invited.

These include tweedy Edith Pilchester, kissed once by Pop at a Christmas party and keen to repeat the experience, and the poor old Brigadier, all frayed cuffs and holey socks, in 'a pair of crumpled corduroys the colour of a moulting stoat', who lives with a commanding sister on milk and Marmite sandwiches. When he creeps over to confide his anxieties about the Gymkhana – Bolshie Fortescue has pulled out of the Committee, pulling his field with him – Pop has it sorted in a flash: they can have his medder, he'll get it mown.

And after a couple of strong snifters, the Brigadier, alongside Mr Charlton, sits down to an al fresco Sunday lunch of roast goose, peas, beans, asparagus, two kinds of potato and Yorkshire pudding, sage and onions, apple sauce and gravy. Mole and Ratty never had it better.

There are mouth-watering meals, and if a Good Sex Award had existed in the Fifties, Bates would surely have won it. Pop in bed on a summer evening, lovingly eyeing Ma's mountains of flesh beneath a transparent nylon nightie; Mr Charlton dissolving as Mariette sits lightly and exquisitely on his lap in a cloud of gardenia scent; their sinking down together in the buttercup field beyond the woods – rarely has desire been rendered so magically. As for the plot, which culminates in (among other things) fireworks, a party after the Gymkhana, and Pop's appalling scheme to turn a country pile to scrap – it is, like the weather, perfick.

I inherited a 1958 second impression of this lovely book from my mother. The jacket is smothered in pink blossom; the yellow Rolls-Royce stands in the yard amongst hens and oil drums; washing flaps gaily on the line. The blurb speaks happily of the 'uninhibited moral code' of the Larkins, facing life 'as many of us would like to face it if we dared'. In the climate of the late Fifties, with the war and rationing not so very far away, this was doubtless true. Read now, in the wake of Sixties excess, and in times of new austerity, with the head of Cameron's 'troubled families unit' chiding feckless women for having too many children, such words sound touchingly innocent, and no less beguiling for that.

My parents adored the novel, as do I. I can still hear my father's roars of laughter as my mother read passages aloud – he particularly liked Ma in her nylon nightie. For all of us it represented the country life we had left when he got a new job in London – carefree happiness, hens round the back door, the mournful old Brigadier: perhaps there was one of those in every Fifties village.

My mother, a compulsive writer who longed above all else to be published, finally wrote to H. E. Bates in 1970 asking his advice, and he responded generously in a hand-written letter. He commended the power of imagination above observation, told her that 'the craft of words must be learned like any other craft – the hard way!' and went on: 'Why not be courageous and send your love affair story to my agent . . . She will give you really professional advice. Even if she didn't want to publish your story she would tell you if your writing had the right sort of style and promise.'

Alas, the agent did not take her on, and the 'love affair story' never saw the light of day, but my mother tucked his letter into the book, and it remains there still.

The Darling Buds of May makes an appearance on a bedside table in SUE GEE's new novel, *Coming Home*, about her parents' return from India in 1947. With luck, it will see the light of day next year.

A Late Victorian Afternoon

MARK JONES

They seemed reasonable enough requests. Don't lie on the bed naked in case passing servants catch an eyeful. Also, in mixed company, could he try to swear only in French? Modest pleas made by Theodore Watts-Dunton to the poet and ex-libertine Algernon Charles Swinburne when they first set up home together. It was 1879 and Swinburne's relish for brandy and flagellation had reached a critical point. In the nick of time, Watts-Dunton, the gallant walrus-moustached solicitor-turned-author, had plucked his friend from the depths and carried him off for a spot of detox in Putney.

The house to which they retreated for the next thirty years lends its name to a witty and evocative book about their lives together. *At the Pines* by Mollie Panter-Downes, first published in 1971, tells, in discursive and observant prose, the story of an intimate if unimpeachably platonic alliance which blossomed in high-ceilinged, over-furnished rooms between two Victorian bachelors.

A contributor to *The New Yorker* for fifty years, Panter-Downes was a Londoner whose pithy reportage of wartime life in the capital first established her reputation as wielder of the skilful phrase and the sardonic punch-line. Although she is nowadays somewhat unjustly forgotten, her considerable body of work (poems, short stories, novels) almost unfailingly invites the reader to relax into the subject in question, assured that this is a writer as able to hold her audience on the metaphysics of rationing as she is on the household by-laws of late nineteenth-century domesticity.

Mollie Panter-Downes, *At the Pines* (1971), is out of print.

Indeed, domesticity of the most reassuring kind is a leitmotiv that runs through every episode of life at The Pines. No surprises or sudden jolts disturb this secluded spot where London's roar fades into the spacious murmur of Putney Hill. Instead we are presented with a veritable demi-paradise wherein Panter-Downes tucks away her two leading characters 'seated side by side, like a couple of hermit crabs of indefinite antiquity', living the quiet life.

Quiet in more ways than one, for both were hard of hearing, and Watts-Dunton's careful stewardship of their tranquil existence (visitors admitted by prior appointment only) ensured that Swinburne's former notorious rambunctiousness had now been reduced to little more than 'the cooing of a dove'. That, at least, was how one of their dinner guests, Max Beerbohm, described the poet's manner of speaking. Seated at table with his hosts in the spring of 1899 he observed Swinburne lost in meditative silence until, once pudding had been served, Watts-Dunton gave his friend the cue to entertain by enquiring how his daily walk had gone. Actually, the enquiry seems to have been more of a bellow, this being what it took to pierce Swinburne's deafness. It appears to have worked, as all present were then treated to a lyrical description of the various natural wonders Algernon had beheld that morning.

Panter-Downes makes young Beerbohm's visit to The Pines the centrepiece of her opening pages, and his nervous anticipation before entering the world of his illustrious hosts would, over sixty years later, find parallels in Panter-Downes's own palpable giddiness at stumbling upon the place quite by chance. Situated, in its early 1970s manifestation, next to a dentist's surgery and a launderette, The Pines' resolutely implacable exterior is likened to 'a widow who has outlived two husbands', with only a commemorative blue plaque pinned to her matronly frontage as a mark of distinction.

Using what one imagines to have been redoubtable powers of persuasion, Panter-Downes soon arranged to go inside and have a look round. Although the interior had by then been split up into flats, there were still some delightful 'incrustations of fustiness and mustiness' which enveloped the place along with 'little clues to the past [which] shyly jogged one's elbow here and there'. In nearly every room she discerns the ghostly strata of days gone by, while out in the garden it feels as if, had she arrived a moment earlier, she would have witnessed those two old friends taking a turn round the flower-beds.

No wonder the spirits of Theodore and Algernon refused to leave. This was the house in which they were for so long free to tend their passions and preoccupations in harmonious seclusion, with only the servants and Watts-Dunton's sister dancing attendance. Here Watts-Dunton was able to beaver away at his novel *Aylwin*, a book so bad as to be almost hallucinogenic (but which, nevertheless, became a contemporary bestseller). Likewise, here Swinburne, the former free-thinking enemy of the 'Galilean serpent', whose erotically charged *Poems and Ballads* had prompted an anonymous correspondent to threaten him with castration, was free to fire off regular letters to the newspapers castigating the French, the Russians, Irish Home Rulers, Uncle Tom Cobleigh and all. Long gone were the days when this diminutive former libertine could be spotted around town tucked under the arm of Sir Richard Burton. By now, Algernon's booze ration was limited to one bottle of beer at dinner. The steadfast Theodore had weaned his friend off the hard stuff.

Not that Watts-Dunton was simply the straight man to Swin-burne's poetic madcap. He was as capable of overpowering ardour as the next man. How else to explain the incident in which he once hid in a hired cab in order to follow a well-known Pre-Raphaelite 'stun-ner', kneeling in the vehicle in case she turned round and spotted him? Such dalliances are, however, as nothing beside Watts-Dunton's passion for gypsies, even the mention of whom brought on a misty-eyed stupor. This fascination seems to have had its origins in a chance encounter with some Romany travellers when he was a boy, and eventually developed into a belief that he was in some way an 'honorary' gypsy himself.

All this talk of gypsies tended to bore Swinburne. Panter-Downes pictures him with eyes glazing over as his friend launches into another extended eulogy on the merits of the Romany life. Not that the tedium flowed all one way. Algernon was a Dickens fan and enjoyed nothing more than giving an after-dinner recital, systematically structured so as to run through the complete works over the course of a recurring three-year cycle, acting out the parts as he went along (Mrs Gamp a speciality). One member of the audience who is on record as having found this especially irksome was a certain Mrs Clara Watts-Dunton. Perhaps a young relation by marriage of the distinguished bachelor?

In fact, somewhat astonishingly, Clara Reich, as she originally was, had, by 1905, become Watts-Dunton's 29-year-old wife. The circumstances surrounding this seismic event are dealt with by Panter-Downes in a wry yet poignant account of a mutual attraction unfettered by age or circumstance. As Clara herself was keen to emphasize in her memoirs, this was no passing crush or gold-digging exercise. Since first accompanying her mother to The Pines as a 16-year-old, Clara had been in love with the courteous old gentleman nearly 44 years her senior.

With the admission of a new member to this exclusive old gentleman's club, it might have been expected that the whole edifice of life at The Pines would crumble. In fact, Swinburne by all accounts accepted Clara from the start. As he got older the poet's childlike ingenuousness seems to have become more and more pronounced so that, in contrast to the empathic bond he enjoyed with Watts-Dunton's young nephew Bertie, most of the other hazily familiar beings he encountered in and around The Pines seemed to form a vague but kindly penumbra of adults around his own second infancy. As Panter-Downes tells it, everyone got on swimmingly. Of course, that entailed some give and take. For every new fixture or fitting Clara introduced, there was a reciprocal obligation to reaffirm Swinburne's right to spout Dickens to the assembled household at six each evening. Household harmony all the way then, until one day in 1909 Algernon went out for his walk and caught a cold which quickly turned into double pneumonia. His death followed soon after, and Watts-Dunton was left as sole heir to his estate. There followed the inevitable skirmishes with the poet's surviving relatives over this posthumous snub. Theodore's detractors came to see him as the philistine gaoler of a poetic genius – a mean and superficial assessment of the real story, according to Panter-Downes.

In any case, by 1914 Theodore himself was past caring, having died that year, and Clara followed her husband at a demure distance in 1938. As soon as they'd all gone, the entire contents of the place were sold off at knock-down prices to a market which had little respect for or interest in their stuffy Victorian provenance.

I first came across *At the Pines* in a local library over thirty years ago. At the time the title sounded to me like some lumberjack's memoir or Scandinavian travelogue. Consequently, it remained on the library shelf and we studiously ignored each other for years. Then one day I picked it up and both of us wondered why it had taken so long. Now it's a book I climb back into from time to time, whenever I want to fetch up in the dainty ambience of a late Victorian afternoon. With Mollie as my formidable guide we pad around the old place unseen by Watts-Dunton, lost in the book-lined thicket of his study, or by Swinburne, back from his daily tramp on Putney Heath and resting (clothed, as per the agreement) on the couch in his room. *At the Pines* is a wonderful book: skilfully written, funny and wryly observant, as well as an ever-ajar door into another world.

MARK JONES is a full-time civil servant and part-time art historian.

The Tortoise of Total War

ANTHONY GARDNER

I don't suppose anyone who buys *Slightly Foxed* can forget the sheer, joyful, all-absorbing intensity with which we read as adolescents; but it took a remark of T. S. Eliot's to bring home to me the pattern of it. Young people, he observed, seldom explore a large number of authors: instead, they tend to seize on a handful of favourites, and try to read everything they ever wrote. For me, one of those authors was Evelyn Waugh: when I came across *Decline and Fall* in my early teens, I wanted to immerse myself for ever in his hilarious, anarchic world where the names alone were enough to bring on fits of help-less laughter. Lady Circumference and little Lord Tangent – not even Dickens could match that combination.

Some of the novels appealed instantly; others took longer to appreciate. *Vile Bodies* seemed the funniest book ever written (it still does), while the romanticism of *Brideshead Revisited* seduced me utterly. But the current of world-weariness in the *Sword of Honour* trilogy was hard to relate to; not until I was a jaded undergraduate did I come to recognize the brilliance of Waugh's most profound and substantial work.

Waugh wrote five novels set during the Second World War, two of them – *Brideshead* and *Put out More Flags* – while its outcome was still in the balance. *Sword of*

Evelyn Waugh's *Sword of Honour* trilogy (*Men at Arms*, 1952; *Officers and Gentlemen*, 1956; *Unconditional Surrender*, 1961) is now available in a single hardback volume: Penguin · 912pp · £30 · ISBN 9780141193557.

Honour took shape over the fifteen years that followed: *Men at Arms* was published in 1952, *Officers and Gentlemen* in 1956, *Unconditional Surrender* in 1961. And yet the trilogy has an immediacy that its predecessors lack. It's fascinating, for those of us who did not experience the war, to see how Waugh's characters react to each new phase of it; and his indignation at the failures of generals and politicians burns across the years.

Sword of Honour follows the military career of Guy Crouchback. Guy is exactly the same age as Waugh – 35 – when hostilities begin, and his experiences are closely based on those of his creator. His personality, though, is completely different. Waugh, according to his friend Randolph Churchill, would have made a very good soldier if he had not so enjoyed driving his superiors mad; Guy is endlessly well-intentioned, with a fatal willingness to take responsibility for others' mistakes.

Men at Arms opens with Guy visiting the tomb of a Crusader, Sir Roger of Waybrooke, before setting out to do his patriotic duty. He is a pious Catholic whose life has been hollow since his divorce from the glamorous, flighty Virginia eight years earlier. The war offers a chance to salvage his self-respect; and just as Charles Ryder's friendship with Sebastian Flyte in *Brideshead* gave him 'a brief spell of what I had never known, a happy childhood', so Guy experiences, as a junior officer in the Halberdiers, 'something he had missed in boyhood, a happy adolescence'.

Like many of Waugh's protagonists, Guy is an innocent, largely passive figure. The character who dominates the book is his fellow trainee Apthorpe, who boasts long years in the African bush and travels with quantities of field equipment, including his 'thunderbox' (a chemical lavatory). Self-absorbed and graceless, he is a source more of wonder than of mirth, but his run-in with his commanding officer is the book's comic fulcrum. Brigadier Ritchie-Hook brims with schoolboy enthusiasm for practical jokes and 'biffing' the enemy, and when he decides to appropriate Apthorpe's thunderbox, the two become locked in a glorious slapstick struggle.

What never ceases to amaze me about *Sword of Honour* is the ease with which Waugh switches back and forth from humour to deep seriousness, or from flights of fancy to stony realism. There are modulations of tone in his earlier books but they are rare by comparison. In this, his final work, Waugh musters the full panoply of his art to demonstrate that nothing is black and white – not even a war against ultimate evil – and no one is entirely predictable. Thus the ghastly Apthorpe acquires a tragic pathos at the end of *Men at Arms*, while the piratical Ritchie-Hooke shows an unexpectedly sentimental side:

> There was a calendar on the chimney piece, rather shabby now in November and coming to the end of its usefulness. Its design was fanciful, gnomes, toadstools, hare-bells, pink bare babies and dragonflies.
>
> 'I say,' he said. 'That's a lovely thing. My word it is lovely. Isn't it lovely?'
>
> 'Yes, sir.'

The book finishes on a subdued note, as Guy's first taste of action – a foolhardy escapade in Dakar – ends with a return to England, his quest for redemption unfulfilled. But the opening of *Officers and Gentlemen* is an altogether different proposition, filled with a wild exuberance that harks back to *Vile Bodies*. The Blitz has hit London, and Waugh's description of it as seen from Guy's club is one of his great comic set-pieces. While the West End burns, the members call for more drinks and bait a hapless Air Marshal who has followed the correct procedure and sought shelter in the billiard room.

> 'D'you know what put me off that last shot?' said Elderbury. 'I trod on someone.'
>
> 'Who?'
>
> 'No one I know. He was under the table and I trod on his hand.'

'Extraordinary thing. Passed out?'

'He said: "Damn."'

'I don't believe it. Parsons, is there anyone under the billiard-table?'

'Yes, sir, a new member.'

'What's he doing there?'

'Obeying orders, he says, sir.'

Two or three bridge-players went to investigate the phenomenon.

What is remarkable about this passage is that Waugh doesn't bother to identify half the characters – but such is his mastery of dialogue that it doesn't matter. Indeed, the lack of definition enhances the effect of cheerful mayhem. He is like a great draughtsman whose most faintly sketched figures in a crowd scene mysteriously contribute to the whole, even though we are scarcely aware of them.

Among the revellers is Tommy Blackhouse, to whose Commando Guy is posted for training on the Isle of Mugg. This episode too is infused with the joyous spirit of early Waugh, though it is closer to *Decline and Fall* than to *Vile Bodies*. Like Paul Pennyfeather negotiating the mad Welsh world of Llanabba Castle, Guy finds himself in a godforsaken spot populated by eccentrics and lunatics – among them the dynamite-loving local laird and 'Chatty' Corner, an old Africa hand revered by Apthorpe:

It was easy to see how he had gained a footing among the gorillas; easy, too, to recognise the English irony in his nickname. He swung his head from side to side, gazing about him from under shaggy brows as though seeking some high path by which he could swing himself aloft and lie cradled in solitude among the rafters.

I love that use of 'high', suggesting not just altitude but the exultation of a primate exploring a beloved habitat: Waugh touchingly dignifies the ape while ridiculing the human being.

The second half of the book brings another change of mood. Guy's chance of heroism seems finally to have come when he is sent into action in Crete. But he arrives to find the battle already lost; the Halberdiers' task is simply to provide cover for the army's retreat. Two characters encapsulate its ignominy: Major 'Fido' Hound, a bureaucrat who goes to pieces under fire, and Ivor Claire, a dashing officer seen by Guy as 'the fine flower of them all', who disobeys orders and sneaks on to one of the last ships out.

Drawing on his own experience of the campaign, Waugh paints a devastating picture of an exhausted and shambolic army, 'the ghosts of formed bodies of troops dragging slowly in the same blind flight'. Yet even here he cannot resist infusing the narrative with lyrical fantasy and even comedy, as in this description of Major Hound on the run:

> He dropped his torch and began feebly to trot. He lost the path and stumbled from boulder to boulder until treading on something which seemed smooth and round and solid in the starlight he found himself in the top of a tree which grew twenty feet below. Scattering Greek currency among the leaves, he subsided quite gently from branch to branch and when he reached the ground continued to roll over and over, down and down, caressed and momentarily stayed by bushes until at length he came to rest as though borne there by a benevolent Zephyr of classical myth, in a soft, dark, sweet-smelling, empty place where the only sound was the music of falling water.

Could any other novelist have served up such a cocktail? I don't think so. Waugh's brilliance is to recognize that a vision of hell can be made all the more effective by interspersing it with glimpses of heaven; and by moving so deftly between light and shade, he is able to confer on the reader the sense of surreal dislocation which possesses the defeated soldiers.

Amid the chaos, Guy preserves a vestige of honour, and manages to escape to Egypt. But Waugh has one last twist of the knife to administer, and he does so – with a touch of genius – through a comic character from *Scoop*, the well-connected Julia Stitch. Afraid that Guy will testify against her friend Ivor Claire, she frustrates his hopes of rejoining his battalion and arranges for him to be sent home by the slowest possible route.

Sword of Honour was not conceived as a trilogy: according to Selina Hastings's excellent biography of Waugh, he originally envisaged four or five volumes. He then changed this estimate to three, before declaring that 'two will do the trick'. But, he admitted in a dust-jacket note to *Unconditional Surrender*, 'This was not quite candid. I knew that a third volume was needed. I did not then feel confident that I was able to provide it.'

Waugh resumes the story in 1943, passing over two 'locust' years which Guy has spent on unsatisfying administrative duties. Britain, to Guy's disgust, has embraced Russia as an ally. 'I should like to do some fighting,' he tells his father. 'But it doesn't seem to matter now who wins.'

Crouchback senior is one of Waugh's most appealing characters: 'an innocent, affable old man who had somehow preserved his good humour – much more than that, a mysterious and tranquil joy – throughout a life which to all outward observation had been overloaded with misfortune'. It is he who provides the trilogy with its spiritual compass. Where *Brideshead Revisited* explored a revelation of Catholic faith, *Sword of Honour* considers how to live by that faith in a world where conspiracy and blind chance seem to have the upper hand.

Both are much in evidence in *Unconditional Surrender*. Conspiracy is represented chiefly by a Communist cell which includes the enigmatic, literary-minded Major Ludovic: a figure whom Waugh manages to make repellent not by drawing him strongly, but by presenting him as a blancmange of a man, impossible to get to grips with. As for chance, Waugh knew better than anyone the humour to be derived from far-fetched coincidences, and here he spins a glittering web of them. All of us, I suspect, have been haunted at some period in our lives by a figure who materializes wherever we go, and Waugh wonderfully encapsulates this phenomenon in the figure of the American officer known as 'the Loot':

> He was in every picture gallery, every bookshop, every club, every hotel. He was also in every inaccessible castle in Scotland, at the sickbed of every veteran artist and politician, in the dressing-room of every leading actress and in every university common-room . . . When Guy went to have his hair cut the Loot seemed always to be in the next chair.

With equal dexterity (and shamelessness) Waugh deploys the figure of a Swahili witch-doctor – 'engaged to cast spells on the Nazi leaders' – who is repeatedly alluded to but only once actually seen. Best and most far-fetched of all is Guy's encounter with a piece of machinery called the Electronic Personnel Selector, explained to him by its operator Mr Oates:

> 'I've been asked to find an officer for special employment; under forty, with a university degree, who has lived in Italy, and had Commando training – one, two, three, four, five –' whirr, click, click, click, click, click. 'Here we are. Now that is a remarkable coincidence.'
>
> The card he held bore the name of A/Ty. Captain Crouchback, G.

The mission for which Guy has been selected – his last of the war – is to liaise with the Communist partisans in Yugoslavia. Here he tries to help a group of Italian Jews make their way home; but as so often, his admirable intentions do more harm than good. At their last meeting the Jews' young spokeswoman tells him,

> 'It seems to me that there was a will to war, a death wish, every-

where. Even good men thought that their private honour would be satisfied by war . . . Were there none in England?'

'God forgive me,' said Guy. 'I was one of them.'

The overriding theme of *Sword of Honour* is the frustration of a soldier's life – and a large part of Waugh's achievement is to convey the tedium created by 'the tortoise of total war' without boring his readers. For every victory or defeat, he reminds us, there are miles of red tape and thousands of men kept in limbo: 'A Kingdom was lost in Europe and somewhere in the Home Counties a Halberdier found himself with his leave stopped, manhandling stores for another move.'

Guy's visit to Sir Roger of Waybrooke's tomb symbolizes his naïve expectations of military glory; and yet the comparison between him and the Crusader is not altogether absurd or ironic. Like a knight in an Arthurian romance, he finds his apparently straightforward quest hedged about with moral ambiguities and unexpected tests. And although almost all his endeavours end in failure, he emerges from them a wiser and a better man – one whom we have come to love. As Eliot put it in his own Second World War epic, *Four Quartets*: 'For us there is only the trying. The rest is not our business.'

ANTHONY GARDNER is profoundly foxed at present, as he is writing a novel about urban foxes and Chinese spies. His previous novel, *The Rivers of Heaven*, contains no wildlife.

The portrait of Evelyn Waugh on p. 34 is reprinted by permission of David R. Godine, Publisher, Inc., from Roberto de Vicq de Cumptich, *Men of Letters & People of Substance*.

Castles in the Air

DAISY HAY

What do an incarcerated minister, an old dressing-up box and a tin of blue paint have in common? They are all central to the plot of *The Swish of the Curtain* by Pamela Brown, a magical children's book, first published in 1941, about a group of friends who take over a disused mission hall and transform it into a theatre.

I have adored *The Swish of the Curtain* since I first read it aged 12, and I'm far from being the novel's only fan. In 2007 Radio 4 broadcast a celebratory documentary on it, featuring contributions from Victoria Wood, Jacqueline Wilson, Maggie Smith, Eileen Atkins, Jenny Eclair and – rather surprisingly – David Bellamy, all of whom credited it with changing their lives. I'm not sure *Swish* changed my life, but it certainly taught me a thing or two about friendship, hard work and ambition – as well as a few handy tips about how to mend a leaky roof, repair a cassock and paint a theatre door blue.

The Swish of the Curtain follows the fortunes of seven children as they embark on an unexpected theatrical adventure. One day, while meandering through the slums of Fenchester (based on Brown's home town of Colchester), the children discover an empty chapel, which has fallen into disrepair following the imprisonment for fraud of its rheumatics-curing minister. With the help of a benign local vicar, the children take over the chapel and turn it into their very own theatre, complete with rudimentary lighting, makeshift dressing-rooms, a rattling stage curtain and a brilliantly blue front door, from which the

Pamela Brown, *The Swish of the Curtain* (1941)
Longwater · Pb · 320pp · £10 · ISBN 9780955242809

theatre and the children's amateur theatrical company derive their names. The novel charts the adventures of the Blue Door Theatre Company as they put on plays and are taken under the wing of a munificent Bishop (the Church of England comes out well in *The Swish of the Curtain*), who takes them to Stratford-upon-Avon and helps persuade their parents to let them train as professional actors.

Like many great children's books, *The Swish of the Curtain* has at its heart an autonomous space that the children make their own. In *Swallows and Amazons* this space is an island; in the William stories it is the Outlaws' Den. Here, however, it is the theatre: a perfectly realized miniature which becomes the children's kingdom. The theatre is the beating heart of *Swish*, and the novel's magic derives in part from the precision with which it is described. Brown shows the steps by which the chapel becomes a theatre very clearly, through careful descriptions of chair-mending, fence-creosoting, backdrop-painting and vigorous floor-scrubbing.

The children think nothing of turning their hand to all these tasks and they are, in fact, impressively multi-talented. Between them they can design a lighting rig, compose a score, produce fabulous costumes, choreograph dances and paint marvellous scenery, and they are all proficient actors. Even Maddy, the 9-year-old baby of the group, can cry on demand, to the envy of her fellow thespians. Their productions are many and various and encompass a range of theatrical disciplines, including comedy, tragedy, ballet and pantomime, before culminating in a hard-hitting contemporary drama, written by the whole group.

The children's talent lends a fairy-tale element to *The Swish of the Curtain*, as does its cast of supporting characters. The vicar is a 'kind fairy, in disguise', who sorts out the theatre's legalities and electricity bills in the twinkling of a clerical eye. Mrs Potter-Smith, meanwhile, is the nearest thing the story has to a wicked witch. The children's only enemy, she drips sweet poison whenever she appears, and the dramatic efforts of her Ladies' Institute, which invariably feature a guest performance by the vicar's hapless curate, provide some great comic set-pieces. Despite her efforts, the children triumph, and the ending is as magical as any lover of fairy-tales could wish.

Central to the novel's charm, however, is that it is very firm about one thing: talent will only get you so far. The children work incredibly hard in order to achieve their dreams, and Brown brilliantly evokes their backstage labours as well as their public triumphs. Lines have to be learned late into the night, the theatre has to be scrubbed and painted in the evenings and at weekends. Some of the children are better actors than others, and the latter have to come to terms with their own limitations. All have to work week after week in order to achieve their separate ambitions. Bulldog, for example, wants more than anything to make the rickety stage curtain 'swish' like the curtain of a real theatre. He trawls the public library for books on the subject, and has to put up with multiple failures before he arrives at a design that works. The moment when the curtain behaves as it should is therefore all the more sweet, particularly as it happens just as the others are beginning to realize that dreams alone may not be enough to turn them into professional actors. That they succeed in making their 'castles in the air' into reality is as much a tribute to effective collaboration and project management as it is to intrinsic talent.

Newton Whittaker

When I first read *Swish*, I found the children's ability to turn fantasy into reality through solid hard work as magical as anything else in the novel, since my own theatrical endeavours never got me beyond some preliminary bossing of my younger sister and the odd programme design. Rereading the novel now, it is evident that it is very much of its time. Appropriately for a book written during the hungry '30s and published during the Blitz, it represents a triumph of imagination over austerity, of make-do-and-mend over big budgets and lavish props. But this also makes it feel surprisingly contemporary. While it might at first appear to be a book about a group of children discovering the limelight, in fact it couldn't be less *X-Factor* or more Big Society. Everything is done on a shoestring, and the children's ambitions are not selfish. They want to become professional actors so they can return to Fenchester and give the town that has helped them a proper theatre, with its own resident company. All of them are thoroughly community-minded, and are loyal both to each other and their town. At one point the Bishop praises them for 'the cultivation of talents for reasons which are not egotistical', and this is an ethos which runs through the novel.

The story also has a nicely feminist bite to it. Although the girls are a credit to their domestic-science teachers, and are dab hands at cooking, sewing and cleaning, they are every bit as ambitious as their brothers, and in some cases considerably more talented. Lynette, in particular, has the makings of a very fine actress, and for her the experience of visiting Stratford with the Bishop is transformative.

I have a particular affection for the Stratford scenes because of the impact they had on my own early experience of Shakespeare. Like the children, the first Shakespeare play I saw was *Twelfth Night*, and I too went to Stratford for the first time to see it (although not, alas, in the company of a benign Bishop). Because I'd read *Swish*, Sir Toby Belch, Sir Andrew Aguecheek *et al.* felt like old friends, and I had an imaginative reference point for the significance of the experience. I didn't want to be an actress when I was 12, but I was well on my way to wanting to be a writer, so I loved reading about the way the children wrote and developed their plays, and I charted my own reactions to literature alongside theirs. I'm not surprised that so many eminent people cite *The Swish of the Curtain* as the book that made them. It demonstrates that you can make your dreams come true, and that if you can make a curtain swish, you can do anything.

DAISY HAY is the author of *Young Romantics: The Shelleys, Byron and Other Tangled Lives* and a Visiting Scholar at Wolfson College, Oxford.

Muddy Boots and a Slouch Hat

CHRISTOPHER ROBBINS

American presidential memoirs have tended to be self-serving tomes, designed to massage reputations and secure their authors a fat windfall on retirement. This was not the case with the first, written by Ulysses S. Grant, who served two terms in the White House (1869–77). Grant does not write about his presidency but about his experiences as the victorious general of the Civil War.

An American friend of mine reads Grant's *Memoirs* every year to remind him of an idealized expression of the American character personified by the old soldier: honest, straightforward, dogged, decent, loyal, self-effacing, courteous and tolerant. Non-Americans are also inspired by the story of a man who in early life failed at everything but who became one of history's great generals.

As a lonely child Grant took refuge in horses, with which he had a natural empathy, and by the time he was 10 he had earned the reputation of someone who could perform equine miracles and ride horses considered impossible. But when, at 16, he was sent to West Point Military Academy, he showed so little aptitude for military tactics that he earned the nickname 'Useless Grant'. Oddly enough, and in spite of a seemingly uncharacteristic penchant for reading romantic novels, it was at West Point that he laid the foundations of his literary style: clean, uncluttered prose that was clear and direct, if poorly spelt.

Not surprisingly, this retiring, taciturn youth had little success

Ulysses S. Grant, *Personal Memoirs* (1885)
Penguin · Pb · 704pp · £12.99 · ISBN 9780140437010

with women until he met the homely Julia who was to become his wife and soulmate. There was never a hint of scandal throughout their long, devoted marriage, although from the beginning Grant's drinking was a problem. It took the form of solitary bingeing in a room with a bottle, followed by punishing hangovers that developed into migraines.

The Mexican-American War of 1846–8 was Grant's first exposure to combat. He demonstrated his personal bravery and superb horsemanship when he volunteered to run the gauntlet during fighting in Monterrey to fetch fresh ammunition. Clinging to the side of his horse with one arm around its neck and one foot draped over the saddle, he rode through a hail of bullets at full gallop. Nevertheless, he thought the war 'one of the most unjust ever waged by a stronger against a weaker nation', and his descriptions of the beauty and grandeur of the country in his *Memoirs* are in sharp contrast to his disgust with the way the US Government treated Native Americans. The experience bred in him a lifelong antipathy to war.

When peace returned, Grant endured a series of dead-end, solitary postings all over the US. Separated from his wife, he was bored and lonely, and his drinking attracted the attention of senior officers. Eventually he was forced to resign from the Army. It was the first of a string of humiliations. Grant now threw all his energy into a variety of ventures, all of which failed. Eventually he was forced to return to work in his father's store in Galena, Illinois.

The Civil War changed Grant's destiny. Recalled to the Army with the rank of Colonel – though he had neither horse nor uniform until a fellow merchant in Galena stumped up for them – he was put in charge of a volunteer rabble that he quickly disciplined into a model regiment. The man who had failed at everything was turning into a formidable commander of men and would eventually become a general of rock-like confidence.

In his muddy boots and black slouch hat, Grant certainly never looked like a general. He always wore a private's uniform with only a general's shoulder tabs to distinguish him. He saw no glamour in combat and felt deeply for the dead and wounded on both sides. He understood the price in blood and misery that victory would demand yet knew that the only purpose of a battle was to win.

The scale of slaughter in the Civil War was first demonstrated at the Battle of Shiloh. It claimed more lives than all previous American wars combined – 30,000 killed, wounded or missing – and it shocked the world. The press, which had always slandered Grant as a drunk, now called him a butcher. The tag stuck and it hurt, but as the war continued and he won battle after battle he was transformed from butcher to victor.

One of my favourite passages in the *Memoirs* is the description of Grant accepting the surrender of the Confederate Army's General Robert E. Lee. Grant rode over to the small house where Lee was installed, arriving as muddy and shabby as ever. Lee, on the other hand, was every inch the General, immaculate in a pale grey uniform with gold braided sleeves, a scarlet sash around his waist, a sword hanging at his side. Grant had left his sword behind – it got in the way when riding, he explained.

The admiration Grant felt for Lee almost amounted to a sense of awe and he did not attempt to hide it. As the staff prepared the surrender documents, the Generals chatted about the Mexican War and mutual military acquaintances. (Lee might have been surprised to learn that one of Grant's most trusted staff officers was a Native American.) Grant became so absorbed in the conversation that Lee finally had to remind him of the business at hand.

Grant did not ask for Lee's sword and added a sentence to the terms of the surrender allowing Confederate officers to retain their side-arms, horses and baggage to avoid unnecessary humiliation. Lee was moved by the gesture. Later, he admitted with embarrassment that his men were starving. Grant immediately agreed to provide 25,000 rations. The following day he rode over again for a long, friendly conversation with his defeated adversary.

The war was over, but it had devastated large areas of the country and killed 625,000 Americans – far more than the United States lost in the Second World War. To add to the trauma President Abraham Lincoln was now assassinated. Grant became the obvious choice for the Republican nomination. He accepted and promptly returned to Galena where his stature was such that he was elected President without going on a campaign tour, making speeches or even appearing much in public.

He was to serve two terms in the White House, and from the beginning his critics accused him of being unschooled in government and ignorant of economics. He was certainly a poor politician, and the White House was rocked by a string of financial and political scandals during his incumbency. As a man of absolute integrity himself, Grant was incapable of detecting dishonesty in those close to him. However, the esteem in which he was held, coupled with his obvious decency, did help to heal the wounds of a nation bloodied and shaken by a terrible war. He brought the South back into the Union and kept America out of two potential foreign wars.

Upon leaving the White House, the President and his wife did not lose their taste for living in style and mixing with the rich and powerful, but there was scant income to support such an expensive life. Money was raised by public subscription to provide the Grants with an annual income. Grant invested it in Mexican railroad bonds, the railroads defaulted and the money was lost.

Grant now decided, implausibly, to make his fortune on Wall Street. Buck Grant, the President's son, had gone into business with a bright young man with the idea of investing money raised from Civil War veterans. With the General as a front, money poured in. The idea was a good one but unfortunately Buck was as big a fool in business as his father. Worse, his partner was a ruthless conman, the Bernie Madoff of his day. He was simply running a Ponzi scheme, using new investments to deliver profits to previous investors, and stealing the rest.

When the scheme eventually collapsed, Grant was left ruined and bitterly humiliated. Mark Twain then suggested that Grant write his memoirs and offered to become his publisher, giving a generous advance and share of the profits.

The *Memoirs* naturally became one of the seminal works of the American Civil War. For me, though, the story of the writing of the book is equally gripping. Before Grant started work he was diagnosed with throat cancer. The diagnosis was a death sentence at the time, guaranteeing a difficult and painful end, but Grant was determined to finish the book before he died. The composition was as brave and arduous an undertaking as any of his military campaigns. He wrote every word himself and used his phenomenal memory instead of a team of researchers to reconstruct with precision each and every battle of the Civil War. Despite being in constant pain, he methodically turned out twenty to fifty pages a day.

There is a wonderful photograph of him at work, wrapped in a blanket with a woollen cap on his head, sitting on his porch in winter in a wicker chair, writing on a pad, pencil in gloved hands. Grant began the book in late 1884 and finished it in July 1885, five days before his death.

Mark Twain immediately knew that he had a great book on his hands. He compared the *Memoirs* to Caesar's *Commentaries*:

Clarity of statement, directness, simplicity, unpretentiousness, manifest truthfulness, fairness and justice toward friend and foe alike, soldierly candour and frankness, and soldierly avoidance of flowery speech. A great, unique and unapproachable literary masterpiece. There is no higher literature than these modest simple memoirs . . .

Unlike modern publishers, Twain did not expect the book to sell itself. An army of 10,000 door-to-door salesmen was recruited, many of them veterans dressed in uniform, and households were offered a wide choice of variously priced bindings. Excluding the Bible, it became the best-selling book in the history of America.

The *Memoirs* have been praised ever since. Even the waspish and anti-military Gore Vidal was an admirer: 'It is simply not possible to read Grant's memoirs without realizing that the author is a man of first-rate intelligence . . . his book is a classic.'

At the very end of the *Memoirs*, with Grant only days from death, this man of war who had failed at everything but soldiering wrote:

I feel we are on the eve of a new era, when there is to be great harmony between the Federal and the Confederate. I cannot stay to be a living witness to the correctness of this prophecy; but I feel it within me that it is to be so. The universally kind feeling expressed to me when it was supposed that each day would prove my last, seemed to be the beginning of the answer to 'let us have peace'.

CHRISTOPHER ROBBINS is currently writing *Blood, Oil and Pomegranates: In Search of Azerbaijan, Land of Fire.*

Mother's Familiar

LAURENCE SCOTT

My parents had no interest in books. Having survived the Second World War, they found everything they needed in each other, and in their north London suburban home with doors they could lock, in a location free from falling bombs. For my father, it was 'real life' that mattered, so the daily and evening newspapers were sufficient; and my mother, as ever, deferred to him. They possessed between them a couple of telephone directories, an ancient *Thorndike* dictionary used by my father for his daily crossword, and the *Radio Times*, which my mother insisted on calling 'the television book', and that was it. Or so I thought.

One afternoon in 1960, when I was a short-trousered 10-year-old, I came home from school and rummaged through the bottom shelf of my mother's kitchen larder, hoping to find some Iced Gems. No luck with the Gems, but in the larder, inside a dusty old pressure-cooker, I found a paperback book in a plain brown-paper wrapper.

I don't know about yours, but in my childhood home a paperback book hidden inside a plain brown-paper wrapper, inside a dusty old pressure-cooker, inside a larder, meant something parental was definitely up: this book was out-of-bounds.

I opened it immediately. It was called *Lady Chatterley's Lover*. I was just about to flick through some pages when my mother entered the kitchen. So I quickly slipped it back inside the plain brown-paper wrapper, inside the pressure-cooker, etc., then gathered myself

D. H. Lawrence, *Lady Chatterley's Lover* (1928)
Penguin · Pb · 368pp · £8.99 · ISBN 9780141192178

sufficiently to divert her attention by muttering something about the Cold War and the Iced Gems shortage.

That evening, I was *en famille* watching the BBC News when a film came up showing the inside of a bookshop in central London, and a queue of customers stretching from the till, out through the doors and along the Charing Cross Road. They were buying copies of *Lady Chatterley's Lover* – each copy thoughtfully covered by the bookshop people in a plain brown-paper wrapper identical to the larder edition. As my mother was a dutiful stay-at-home housewife, and my father commuted daily to his work in central London, I assumed the book must be his.

I looked across the room to a column of blue-grey pipe smoke and wondered if my father was in there. Mustering an innocent tone, I asked the smoke what the book on television was about.

'Ask your mother,' said the smoke.

I did. She pursed her lips.

While my mother oozed silent disapproval from every pore, Rowley, her elderly familiar, cunningly disguised as a Pekingese asleep on her lap, suddenly looked in my direction and uncovered its one remaining tooth – a glinting canine. I took the hint and backed off.

Silence was my parents' default response to anything connected with, or even remotely alluding to, sex and bodies. Their only apparent interest in these topics was in acquiring the techniques necessary to avoid them. So the moment my parents clammed up was the moment I knew what the book was about.

At the time I didn't know that Penguin Books, the publishers of D. H. Lawrence's *Lady Chatterley's Lover*, had recently been prosecuted at the Old Bailey under the Obscene Publications Act of 1959. You will probably remember that they had attempted to publish an uncensored edition, but it was argued that the book's explicit depiction of sexual intercourse would deprave and corrupt its readers. However, under the Act, if it could be proved that the book was 'of literary merit', Penguin would escape prosecution and the novel could deprave and corrupt its readers with impunity.

A whole bunch of literary and intellectual heavyweights came to the book's defence, including E. M. Forster and Helen Gardner. The trial touched the national *Zeitgeist* of emerging post-war liberalism and the demise of deference, and for several weeks it became a daily regular in all the mainstream media. Hence, when the book was declared 'not guilty', the cameras were there to record the moment of liberation.

After the larder discovery, I lay awake for hours buzzing with the excitement of forbidden knowledge and resisting the desire to know more. At around 9.30 p.m. desire won out. I rose from my bed and, on the pretext of needing a glass of milk in order to prevent 'night starvation', went down to the kitchen.

While my parents were watching television, I slipped the book beneath my dressing-gown, nipped up the stairs and, once safely between the sheets, began to read while tucking into milk and Iced Gems. (They were in the cheese dish.) Coincidentally, and with the help of my father's *Thorndike*, I had recently conducted an exhaustive study of sex words and concluded they were four in number, five at a pinch, seven if you allowed hyphens.

After an age of concentrated effort I located most of the sex words but also found that they were surrounded by lots of other words which complicated matters to such a degree that whole sections of the novel were completely beyond comprehension. In fact, apart from one or two body parts, I could barely make any sense of it at all. My father had obviously had difficulty too, because he had marked with his crossword pencil all the passages requiring further study.

I became very unsettled and took to staring up at the ceiling in a kind of reverie of reassessment. Could it really be that my father had bought a book? Could he, who wore a two-piece suit, cardigan, white shirt and tie every day of his life and never revealed so much as a bare forearm, be interested in bodies? And what about this sex thing? If he was interested in sex, then it was likely that he did whatever it was with my mother, and that was totally unacceptable. They were Mum and Dad and I was the centre of their universe, a place I intended to occupy forever, but now a hinterland of half-guilt, half-innocence. Like L. P. Hartley's uncomfortable narrator in *The Go-Between*, I found myself 'ignorant of the language, yet compelled to listen'.

Confused and indignant, I decided to return the book to the larder and never say another word. Like my father I would be silent, and he would be none the wiser. He would be, that is, if it wasn't for Rowley.

Rowley was an aristocratic curmudgeon with a Crufts prize-winning pedigree set out in official Kennel Club documents. They described him as a 'lion type' Pekingese, presumably because his appearance resembled the mane of a lion that had suffered a scalping. Detached from its host, this elliptical mass of golden tresses, complete with centre parting, had developed a hidden and inexplicable means of propulsion, enabling him to float about the house in a silent and uncanny manner not dissimilar to a hovercraft. But because the head end was indistinguishable from the non-head end, it was virtually impossible to ascertain if he was in forward gear, or if he was manoeuvring in reverse. At night he slept on his favourite rug at the foot of the stairs, where, until 10 p.m., he permitted everyone free passage up and down the stairs as they wished, but from 10 p.m. until 6.30 the following morning – the time when my mother would rise to use the bathroom – he refused to allow anyone down.

Time now, 11.15 p.m.

Clutching *Lady Chatterley's Lover* under my dressing-gown, I descended on tip-toe to the penultimate stair, focused on the sleeping golden tresses and peered in. I looked for the non-head end and gingerly placed a naked foot beside it.

The pain could be likened to an ice-pick inserted behind an ankle tendon, then levered from side to side. He growled, I screamed. He shook his head, I fell to the floor where we kicked up a heck of a racket. The plain brown-paper wrapper flew in one direction, the book in another.

I looked up to see both parents looking down. From the top of the stairs their half-awake gaze tried to make sense of the scene, eventually focusing on the book's front panel, its title apparent to all. Without so much as a change of expression, they went silently back to their room.

At 6.29 a.m. I returned to the penultimate stair.

At 6.31 a.m. I returned the book to the pressure-cooker.

From that day on, my parents and I operated our very own *Chatterley* ban, and by some strange process of tacit consent, the book was never mentioned again.

Several decades later, after my mother's death, I was clearing out some of her belongings and was surprised to find on her bedside table – in addition to a photographic portrait of Rowley in a cardboard frame bearing the unlikely legend 'Gone to Heaven', and some pencils propped up in an old jam-jar – a current library membership card.

I was even more surprised to find the cupboard below stuffed full with yellowing paperbacks, mostly from the 1960s: Edna O'Brien's *The Country Girls*, Henry Miller's *Tropic of Cancer*, Doris Lessing's *The Golden Notebook* . . . My first thought was that they belonged to my father, but on flicking through the pages I discovered a scattering of pencilled marginalia, underlinings, notes, reminders, comments – all in my mother's hand. And at the very bottom of the cupboard, beneath all the other books, still in its brown-paper wrapper, was that same old copy of *Lady Chatterley's Lover*. The pencilled underlinings and marked passages were just as I remembered them, but more had been added: single exclamation marks, individual words circled, my mother's impatient half-formed comments on Lawrence's sexism.

The books were hers, and so were the marks, probably made with one of the pencils I have on my desk, propped up in an old jam-jar.

LAURENCE SCOTT, an occasional poet and teacher, lives in south-west Scotland where he is writing a memoir, *Train Passing Through*. His poems pop up in various magazines and journals.

Comfortable Words

ANTHONY WELLS

When I was working at the Wiener Library (the research institute for the study of Nazism and the persecution of the Jews) in the 1980s, after the original collection had been transferred to Tel Aviv, we began to solicit bequests and donations of books from people who might have titles of relevance to us. For the first time in living memory there were empty shelves waiting to be filled. So the chief librarian and I began our tour of north-west London, of Highgate and Hampstead, Hendon and St John's Wood ('Hephzibah . . . only wished she could find a reference in the Bible to God's covenant with English Jews, promising them St John's Wood High Street,' wrote Howard Jacobson in *The Finkler Question*) – visiting the flats and houses of the lucky few, the exiles and refugees and survivors, to scour their libraries.

These ranged from the scholarly and exhaustive, where tomes in German, French, Italian, Hebrew, Russian and English lined the studies and sitting-rooms, to simple glass-fronted bookcases containing little more than the works of Goethe and Schiller. What a comment it was on the ignorance and malignity of the Nazis that they should have harried, abused and driven out a people who so prized the great figures of German culture.

We had no place for Goethe and Schiller but we took their selected and collected works, their biographies and correspondences and anthologies, as the price to be paid for the rare finds we were

---

The 1662 *Book of Common Prayer* is published in various editions by the Cambridge University Press.

after – a collection of Friends of Europe pamphlets from the 1930s, perhaps, or a run of Leopold Schwarzschild's *Neue Tagebuch* (published in exile from Paris) – in the way someone who only likes strawberry creams has to buy the whole tin of Quality Street. I took advantage of the ballast that came in to boost my own modest book collection, offering a few pence for items outside the library's remit and of no resale value to it: Heine's *The Romantic School*, maybe, or Victor Mollo's *The Complete Bridge Player*.

Just once or twice we came upon a treasure trove, in German-Jewish terms the equivalent of the Amber Room; and it was from one of those that Kurt Hahn's copy of the *Book of Common Prayer* came into my possession.

As I recall, it arrived with the library of Robert Weltsch, one of the richest collections that came our way in those years. Weltsch had been a leading figure in the German Jewish community of the Thirties, editor of the *Jewish Review* and author of a defiant leading article there in April 1933 entitled 'Wear the yellow badge with pride'. He got out to Palestine in 1938 and eventually settled in England. Originally from Prague, Weltsch when younger had been a member of the Czech-German-Jewish circle which included Franz Werfel, Max Brod and Franz Kafka. So it was no surprise that his library contained plenty of these writers' works, many with pencilled annotations, and with clippings and scribbled notes stuffed between their pages. These books (perhaps signed by their authors) had not accompanied their owners into exile – how could they have? – but in handling the volumes and scanning the handwritten notes, you certainly felt you were connecting with a past world, a cultural, intellectual, literary, social world now lost and gone for ever, except in memory.

To find the *Book of Common Prayer* among the collection was a surprise. To discover the name of Kurt Hahn – the founder of Gordonstoun and originator of Outward Bound – stamped on the inside cover, an even greater one. There was the intriguing, if minor, question of how a book of Hahn's had found its way into Robert

Weltsch's library, but that may not have been so odd: Hahn was also part of the German-Jewish diaspora in Britain, even if not connected to the Prague circle (although he was descended from a Grand Rabbi of Prague on his mother's side). Weltsch had been director of the Leo Baeck Institute in London, whose purpose was to recover the history of the German Jews; no doubt Kurt Hahn had been interested in its work. He probably contributed to it, perhaps providing a memoir of how he had protested against Hitler's assumption of power in 1933, been briefly imprisoned, struggled to keep his boarding-school at Salem going through the first year of the Third Reich, and then, recognizing the impossible, left the German tyranny behind and moved to Britain to re-found his school in a new setting.

So was this the Gordonstoun headmaster's *Book of Common Prayer*, the one he took to chapel with him every day – and twice on Sundays – as my own headmaster had taken his twenty years previously? It was the familiar chunky vingesimo-quarto size, printed on India paper, gilt-edged, with marbled endpapers, and bound in a green-tinged soft leather which made it comfortable, and comforting, to hold.

> Hear what comfortable words our Saviour Christ saith unto all who truly turn to him.

What had been Hahn's relationship to Christianity? He converted in 1945, according to the *Dictionary of National Biography*. Had he believed, or accepted, that to run a boarding-school in this country you needed the established religion to be part of it, and so readily conformed to its practices himself? After all, he was educating the sons of Albion now. I suspect that our own headmaster took a similar view. Better they should be raised in this religion than none at all; and as well this religion as another. In Hahn's case, perhaps he shared Claude Montefiore's liberal Jewish view that Christianity also revealed truths about the nature of God.

We tended not to use our own prayer-books at school: there were standard-issue ones waiting for us in the chapel pews, along with *Hymns Ancient and Modern*. At home in the holidays, however, when, before rebellion set in, I trooped off to Matins with the family on Sunday mornings, I would self-importantly carry one of my father's copies of the *Book of Common Prayer* to church. It was in the same bulky, weighty format, with a similarly soft cover, as Kurt Hahn's. No wonder the book stirred memories when it fell into my hands.

Not just the book. From years of repetition, many of the passages of this prayer-book were sewn into the lining of my memory, and a mere glance at the familiar friable pages brought them back. Confessions, creeds and collects were implanted in my mind, their language indissolubly entwined with any attempt to address the Almighty or express those emotions – of humility, gratitude for life, confession of ignorance, acceptance of mortality – that are largely the preserve of religion.

> Almighty and most merciful Father, we have erred and strayed from thy ways like lost sheep. We have followed too much the devices and desires of our own hearts. We have offended against thy holy laws . . .

As it happened, it was around the time the Weltsch collection arrived that I started to go to church again, after a gap of seventeen years. The return was driven partly by personal difficulties but also by an inability to find satisfactory answers to the problems posed by the place where I was working. The Wiener Library was full of paradoxes, the central one being that it existed to preserve the record of one of the greatest crimes in human history. At one moment I was assembling exhibition material on Kafka – all three of whose sisters, Gabriele, Valerie and Ottilie, died in the 'great destruction' – the next I was reshelving a massive bound volume of *Das Schwarze Korps*, the SS weekly. At every turn one was confronted by the evidence of something so heinous it defied belief. The Dutch pastor Visser't Hooft expressed the contradiction well: 'From that moment onwards I had no excuse to shut my mind to information which could find no place in my view of the world and humanity.'

It was at the moment I realized I was unable to comprehend the events the Library documented that I picked up Kurt Hahn's *Book of Common Prayer* and returned to the religious liturgy of my youth. The sinew, rhythm, gravity and plain-speaking of its prose were a great balm. The effect was a faint echo of that of the Easter church bells on Goethe's despairing Faust:

> *Und doch, an diesen Klang von Jugend auf gewöhnt,*
> *Ruft er auch jetzt zurück mich in das Leben.*
> (And yet from childhood up familiar with the note,
> To Life it now renews the old allegiance.)

And so on one of the following Sundays I took Kurt Hahn's *Book of Common Prayer* and headed off for the morning service at St Marylebone Parish Church.

As it turned out, though, I was too late. Not for the service; too late for the *Book of Common Prayer*. While I had been away, the liturgy had been rewritten. Matins, for so long the main Sunday morning service, Holy Communion being reserved for pious early risers at 8 a.m., had been replaced by something called the Eucharist. And on the service sheet, after the heading Choral Eucharist, were printed the words 'Series 1 & 2 revised'.

Back in the pews, unsuspecting, I tried to recite what I knew by heart, but it no longer chimed with what was being declaimed from the chancel.

> The Lord be with you
> *And with thy spirit*

had become

> The Lord be with you
> *And also with you.*

I persevered for a few more Sundays until I finally got the message: the *Book of Common Prayer* was no longer the book of common prayer, it was one alternative among several, and the least favoured. With it had gone, among other prized things,

> Then shall the Priest, turning to the people, rehearse distinctly all the TEN COMMANDMENTS

– to quote from the second page of the old Communion service. Did Kurt Hahn feel that there at least the new religion he had embraced was a proper continuation of the old? It is a simple thought, but one that struck me often enough as I reshelved Nuremberg Trial documents, or passed the great map on the wall of the Library's entrance hall which recorded the toll of Jewish victims in the various countries of Europe, that if more Germans had obeyed the second of the commandments which God gave to Moses –

> Thou shalt love thy neighbour as thyself

and the sixth –

> Thou shalt do no murder

– there might have been no reason for the Wiener Library, no reason either for Kurt Hahn to have left Salem for Scotland, and hence no reason for his copy of the prayer-book – still with me to this day – to have ended up in the hands of a lapsed Anglican modern linguist.

ANTHONY WELLS worked for many years as librarian and translator at the Institute of Contemporary History and Wiener Library in London, and before that for the BBC Monitoring Service covering first East Germany, then southeastern Europe. He now divides his time between writing and running a small business.

Woon, Wordy-Major and Wootz

JOHN KEAY

Dictionaries, encyclopaedias and the like are best browsed at leisure; approach them with an open mind and prepare for the unexpected. The entry sought may confirm or confound one's expectations but greater enlightenment generally lurks elsewhere on the page. As with companions of any sort, the test of a compendium lies in the extent to which it diverts.

So I looked up – as one does – 'Writer'. The entry contained no mention of penmanship and offered just two rather predictable definitions – predictable, that is, in a nineteenth-century work subtitled *A Glossary of Colloquial Anglo-Indian Words and Phrases and of Kindred Terms, Etymological, Historical, Geographical and Discursive*.

The first definition of Writer gave 'the rank and style of the junior grade of covenanted civil servants of the East India Company' and the second 'any copying clerk in an office, native or European'. No surprises there, then, although from the two columns of etymological examples that followed much could be gleaned about the covenanted writer's lifestyle: it was 'not a little scandalous', often

---

Hobson-Jobson, A Glossary of Colloquial Anglo-Indian Words and Phrases, and of Kindred Terms, Etymological, Historical, Geographical and Discursive by A. C. Burnell and Henry Yule (1886; 2nd edition edited by William Crooke, John Murray, 1903, and Routledge and Kegan Paul, 1985), is available as a Cambridge University Press paperback (2010 · 928pp · £45 · ISBN 9781108018395). *Hanklyn-Janklin or A Stranger's Rumble-Tumble Guide to Some Words, Customs and Quiddities Indian and Indo-British* (1992) by Nigel B. Hankin is available in a new edition from India Research Press, New Delhi, 2003 and 2008.

rather short, began early (James Forbes was just 16 when he stepped ashore at Bombay), could lead either to a military commission (e.g. Lord Clive) or neglect of the Company's business in favour of one's own (just about everyone), and it often engendered, especially in Madras, 'exceeding pride and the knack of forgetting old acquaintances'. The same might be said of many later writers, covenanted or not. My eye strayed on. At the bottom of the page 'Writer' was followed by an entry on 'Wug', and on the facing page it was preceded by 'Woon', 'Wordy-Major' and 'Wootz'. I'd never heard of any of them. They proved irresistible and so, in time, did the book.

Hobson-Jobson, to give it its better-known title, has now been a friend for twenty years. As a bedtime browse it replaced Bill Dalton's *Indonesia Handbook* in around 1990. (Originally a serendipitous companion to the archipelago's 1,700 islands, and larded with helpful tips on the availability of hashish, Dalton's work has been much reissued and is now not as quirky as it was.) I can't remember how I came by *Hobson-Jobson*. A quote from it appears on page one of my first book (*Into India*, 1973) but my only copy is a 1985 reprint of the second edition (1903) with a new foreword by Anthony Burgess.

 The first edition appeared in 1886 under the joint authorship of A. C. Burnell and Henry Yule. Burnell was a Sanskrit-minded member of the Madras Civil Service who died before publication and Colonel Sir Henry Yule was a dapper Scots soldier-scholar who, from retirement in Palermo, produced *Cathay and the Way Thither* for the Hakluyt Society and a magisterial edition of *The Travels of Ser Marco Polo*. Lexicography followed and, as well as *Hobson-Jobson*, Yule contributed substantially to James Murray's work on what became the *Oxford English Dictionary*.

'My first endeavour in preparing this work has been to make it accurate,' says Yule in his foreword to *Hobson-Jobson*, 'my next to make it interesting.' Its accuracy has sometimes been questioned.

Burgess, for instance, cocks an eyebrow over the notion that 'I don't give a damn' was originally 'I don't give a dam'. Since a dam was an Indian copper coin of infinitesimal value, the entry claims that 'whatever profanity there may be in the animus, there is none in the etymology'. So it was not the Duke of Wellington who, so to speak, coined the phrase; he merely turned it into an oath with the addition of an 'n'. Yet no examples are forthcoming to show that English writers, even covenanted ones, ever did actually give a 'dam' about anything.

Accuracy succumbs to conjecture – regarding bananas, 'it can hardly be accidental', we're told, that the Arabic for fingers and toes is *banan* – yet the interest never flags. What Yule calls 'divagations' from the original project account for a richness of subjects that 'may seem hardly to come within the scope of a glossary'. Thus, in north India, sauce for the goose is definitely not sauce for the 'Ganda', this being a corruption of the Sanskrit word for a rhinoceros. On the other hand 'bamboo', a word 'of exceedingly obscure origin' yet 'one of the commonest in Anglo-Indian use', has become as naturalized as 'the gigantic grass' to which it applies.

We learn, too, of linguistic oddities like 'the principle of degradation', a trickle-down effect whereby titles decline in estimation from being terms of respect to terms of familiarity and finally of contempt. 'Bibi', for example, once denoting the consort of a nawab, then any wife, had by the late nineteenth century degenerated into a euphemism for a prostitute. Converting Hindi imperatives into quasi-English infinitives was another peculiarity of Anglo-Indian usage. 'Puckerow' and 'Dumbcow', properly *pakarao* and *damkhao* meaning 'apprehend him' and 'silence him', came to serve as English verbs and even nouns. Yule thinks this may 'exemplify some obscure linguistic law'. More obviously it exemplifies the imperialists' imperious behaviour.

All the usual English borrowings from the East are here – gingham, dungarees, loot, bungalow, dinghy, typhoon, mandarin, shawl – and a good few that are less usual. 'Bobbery-bob', an interjection at times of stress, apparently derives from *Bapre bap*, 'O Father, Father'. It was often to be heard at executions. Similarly 'Hobson-Jobson' itself, meaning 'a native festal excitement' ('it's just some local Hobson-Jobson'), is supposedly a bowdlerization of '*Ya Hasan, Ya Hosain*', the Muslim cry that accompanies the breast-beating processions at Muhurram. Yule explains that the term was chosen as the title of the book on the grounds that it was more memorable than the wordy description that became the subtitle and that it 'conveyed a veiled intimation of dual authorship'.

It has also stuck, been imitated and become a generic term for any dictionary of hybrid words and cross-cultural customs. *Hanklyn-Janklin or A Stranger's Rumble-Tumble Guide to Some Words, Customs and Quiddities Indian and Indo-British* was first published in 1992. A post-colonial sequel to *Hobson-Jobson*, it gives pride of place to Indian usages of English words rather than English usages of Indian words and will be found invaluable when trying to read an English-language Indian newspaper for the first time. The author, Nigel Hankin, a soldier who stayed on in India after Independence, explains the title with the assertion that 'jingle or echo words' ('party-warty', 'booky-wooky' etc) are much employed in an affectionate context within English-speaking Indian families; 'the echo usually begins with a *wa* sound', which would result in 'Hanklyn-Wanklin', but this 'could seem a little outré', says Hankin. Better might be 'Hankin-Pankin'. It's more in the spirit of 'Hobson-Jobson' and could be validated on the same jingly grounds as 'rumble-tumble', the Indian army slang for scrambled eggs ('but of no great age since it is not mentioned in *Hobson-Jobson*').

Hankin draws attention to a review of *Hobson-Jobson* that appeared in Lahore's *Civil and Military Gazette* in 1886. It was written by the young Rudyard Kipling, one of that paper's two staff reporters, and it correctly foretold a great future for Yule and Burnell's book: 'unless we are much mistaken, it will take its place  among the standard works on the east; and will pass, gathering bulk as it goes, from decade to decade'. Kipling's only criticism related to the entry on the 'Doombur', otherwise the *doomba* or *dumba*, the sheep of Afghanistan that has a fat tail which, like the book, 'gathers bulk as it goes'. Despite packing his entry with references to the tail gathering so much bulk that a small wheeled cart was needed to support it, Yule had been unable to find any evidence that this practice was ever in fact the case. Kipling set him right; outside his office there was just such a ram wandering the streets of Lahore towing its tail in a two-wheeled barrow.

Scrupulous attention to details of no conceivable importance is what distinguishes both works. Thus, in case you're wondering, 'Wootz' turns out to be 'an odd name that has attached itself in books to the so-called natural steel of S. India but . . . has never since [1795] been recognised as the name of steel in any language and would seem to be a clerical error'; 'Woon' is merely a phonetic spelling of *wun*, the Burmese name for a governor or any other administrative officer; a 'Wordy-Major' is 'a native adjutant of Indian Irregular cavalry' (though 'both the rationale of the compound title and the etymology of *wardi* are obscure'); and 'Wug' is the same as *bag*, being either the Sindi or Baluchi word for 'loot' – or rather for 'a herd of camels', they being the normal form of loot in what is now south-west Pakistan. And so on – for just over 1,000 pages. *Hobson-Jobson* has indeed passed from decade to decade, ensuring for the insomniac bibliophile long nights of worthless but never boring diversion.

JOHN KEAY co-edited with Julia Keay the *Collins Encyclopaedia of Scotland* and the current edition of Macmillan's *London Encyclopaedia*. Unlike Henry Yule, he did not have to handwrite the entire text of either of these books four times. The illustrations in this article are from *Hanklyn-Janklin*.

Shelf Life

YSENDA MAXTONE GRAHAM

Banishment, destruction, murder and deportation are, regrettably, an integral part of good housekeeping – especially if you live in a small house, as I do. Banishment is putting things up in the attic for a generation. Destruction is dismantling Lego creations which no one has played with for a month. Murder is throwing things away. Deportation is taking things to charity shops.

Yesterday I went on a culling spree in my own house, armed with two cardboard boxes for books. I was in a bloodthirsty mood. As I crept about, earmarking books for instant deportation, blowing the thick dust off them as a kindness before saying goodbye to them for ever, I wondered whether other book-lovers did as I did, and what it felt like, and how other people chose which books to get rid of. Do some people never cull their books? I wondered. Do they really keep every single one, treating all books as sacred, even the Dorling Kindersley *Sew Step by Step*? They must need to build a yard of new shelving every year.

'You must be cruel to be kind,' gardeners tell you, about pruning roses. 'The more you cut them down, the more they love it.' This might be true of roses but is it true of book collections? I should imagine they absolutely hate it. Or perhaps the ones that survive are so relieved that they turn a blind eye to the atrocities going on further down the shelf.

'Cull' has a different etymology from 'kill'. I checked – online, not in the *Oxford Dictionary of Etymology*, a worrying new habit. 'Kill' comes from the OE *cwellen*. 'Cull' comes from the gentler French word *cueillir*, which just means 'pick' or 'select', though both soon begin to sound like euphemisms used by Fascist dictators. The poor 'selected' items still end up wrenched out of their homes and carted off to Oxfam or Cancer Research, or whichever of the ten charity shops in your high street happens to be the most convenient for parking.

The skill is to get rid of books which you know for certain nobody will ever miss. (As an author, you must be prepared to face the fact that this very unmissability has been accorded to your own volumes, which you can see for sale on Abe Books, 'used, in very good condition', for £0.64.) First to go, yesterday, were the books called 'Britain's' or 'London's' or 'England's' Lost Something – *Britain's Lost Railways*, *London's Lost Heritage*, *England's Lost Houses*. The loss of these *Losts* will not be felt in this household, I'm pretty certain. They were lost already, as it were. Next to go were books called the Strangest Something. *London's Strangest Tales*, *Railway's Strangest Journeys*, *The Law's Strangest Cases*. The strangeness they contained was diverting for a time, but the novelty soon wore off.

It's shameful to admit it, but all those books were once presents – as so many of the books one selects for culling tend to have been. A kind and generous person once thought that we (or one of our more anoraky children) would enjoy each of those books. Which we did, for a while. Through my head, at the moment of throwing the book into the cardboard box, went the thought, 'I didn't spend my own money on that book, so it won't hurt *me* to get rid of it.' A horribly uncharitable thought, especially on a charity-shop day. I assuaged my guilt by deciding such presents were probably hurriedly bought. Waterstones, 21 December 1998, man with credit card who wanted to get it all done in one day. And at least I wasn't going to sell the books on eBay and make money out of someone else's present. But what if the book was inscribed to you, in large handwriting, with love and kisses from the named friend or relative? Much harder to get rid of, in that case. Word might get round.

There's a certain kind of book that none of us buys for ourselves but we all give to everyone else. The book on the history of the

Ordnance Survey, *Map of a Nation*, is one such. Brilliant idea, wish I'd written it myself, perfect for uncles, aunts, grannies and grandfathers, sons and daughters-in-law. I definitely gave it to people. Our copy is clinging on, taking up four inches of space, not yet read, supposed to be excellent, but so *long*; will its moment ever come? Will I actually ever say, 'Today is the day when I get stuck into *Map of a Nation*'? Let alone 'Can't talk: just finishing *Map of a Nation*'? Its time might be running out. *Cambridge: Treasure Island in the Fens* is another such well-meant book; and *The Lore of the Land: A Guide to England's Legends*.

Then there are the Booker Prize winners from the 1980s. *Oscar and Lucinda* by Peter Carey was plucked yesterday. A big puff of dust came off that one, and into the box it went. Ugly white-spined paperback: good riddance. Next to it was *East of Wimbledon* by Nigel Williams, and that was sucked into the vortex, too. Death by association. They made room for more recent Booker and Costa Prize winners which can now have their turn, but for how long?

It's more painful to get rid of books one has paid good money for – buying them in hardback when they first came out – but which have proved disappointing. Late Martin Amis novels (can't make head or tail of them); *The Finkler Question* (bewilderingly unfunny; is it my problem or his?); *White Teeth* (starts well but goes on far too long). But surely there's no point in having these books grinning down at you from the shelves, mocking your extravagance, when they could be adopted by another family who might give them the love they crave if not deserve.

People say that middle-aged women become 'invisible'. We no longer get whistled at by builders, etc. Middle-aged books become 'invisible' too. So much so that you go for decades without realizing you have multiple copies of them. An English graduate married to another one, I found we had three dog-eared paperback copies of *Sir Gawain and the Green Knight*. ('NB assonance' marked in the margins.) Plus two identical Penguin editions of *The Mayor of*

Casterbridge. ('NB Character is fate, cf Gk trag.') No culling dilemma there – except whose to get rid of. Multiple copies of the Arden *Hamlet*, perhaps, have to be kept, in case you ever host a play-reading, which is unlikely but just possible.

What about the great show-off books which we all had to be seen to be reading when they were published? *Citizens* by Simon Schama; *Mao: The Unknown Story* by Jung Chang and her husband; *Florence Nightingale* by Mark Bostridge; Peter Ackroyd's *Dickens*; Humphrey Carpenter's *Robert Runcie*. Most of us have a shelf of trophy hardbacks like these; as you peruse them it's like being on the ground floor of Hatchards a few years back. Culling these handsome trophies is not easy. They do furnish a room. But the small house

Anna Trench

demands it; and to be honest, that Mao book was a disappointment after *Wild Swans*, wasn't it? Joint authors are never a good idea.

What about inherited books? My Hungarian grandfather left me his collection of books in French and German. So, taking up a great deal of prominent space, I have Heine's Werke, Goethe's Werke, Lessing's Werke, Grillparzer's Werke and Schiller's Werke, as well as the complete Oeuvres of Molière, Corneille and Zola. What to do about these? It's absurd that they should survive, decade in, decade out, when most of the German ones are in Gothic script, which I never learned to read and do not intend to. But the sentimental value is strong, and the books certainly look impressive. Tiny culls have taken place when no one was looking – for example, an uncut Zola paperback which even my grandfather can't have read.

What about recipe books? You must take action if the recipe bookshelf gets so full that you can't prise a book out with greasy fingers. Yesterday I took the step of divesting ourselves of Heston Blumenthal's *The Fat Duck Cookbook*. It had amused us for three years with its recipes for snail porridge and sardine-on-toast sorbet, but I decided enough was enough. We were never, ever going to cook from the thing. I also got rid of a 1990s book of pasta dishes which explained, rather blushingly and with lots of exclamation marks, that 'spaghetti puttanesca' literally meant whore's spaghetti. Very old-hat. But Mary Berry's eternally useful, margarine-based *Ultimate Cake Book* survived, complete with its recipe for 'New Year Tipsy Cake'.

Culling children's books is tricky, because children are upset if they discover that anything has gone, even if they didn't love it much when it was there. But I've become an expert. Go up to their room when they're out. Open the window. Sift through the books which are lying horizontally because they're too tall to stand up in the shelf. They're the annoying ones. You'll be amazed how many of them are called *The History of Britain* or variations on that title. Then there are at least four books on kings and queens. You only need one of these. And if you've got *Our Island Story* plus *1066 and All That*, you've really got all you need for a lifetime's love of British history.

The keeping of the library of a small house, like the keeping of a small garden, is a matter of constant pruning, preening and thinning. You keep (at least I do) the complete Waugh, Wodehouse, Austen, George Eliot, Tolkien, Osbert Lancaster, Conan Doyle, Boswell and Thurber. You keep anything you ever won as a school prize (we have precisely three of those; one of them is *Our World in Colour*). You keep (we do, anyway) every miniature musical score you have ever bought, a burgeoning row of yellowness. The culling only makes things better. The good books stay; the less good ones go; and one day you will have the perfect small book collection, consisting only of books you really might want to read again.

YSENDA MAXTONE GRAHAM's latest book, *An Insomniac's Guide to the Small Hours*, is published by Short Books in what is ominously described as 'gift format'.

The Asterisk Club

BRUCE HUNTER

I met Pamela Branch only once, at a dinner party given by the literary agent David Higham and his wife. Pamela was strikingly beautiful, with large eyes, curious as a cat's. The talk turned to an author
whose new novel was getting a lot of attention and I remarked that
her husband had recently died. 'How did she do it?' asked Pamela
with interest, 'Poison, was it?'

Pamela had already published her fourth novel, *Murder's Little
Sister*, which begins,

> The yellow cushion looked too frivolous in the oven, so Enid
> Marley went and fetched a black one. That did not look right
> either, but it could not be helped. Since she had no intention
> whatever of dying, she was determined to make herself as
> comfortable as possible . . .
>
> She had thought it all out with great care, planned each
> detail, revised it, scrutinized it from every angle. She knew well
> that it was a drastic ploy, but it was the only one left untried.
> Somehow, she had to recapture her husband. It was not that she
> loved nor even liked him, but to be deserted by no less than
> three men – all of whom had quite frankly married her for her
> money – was ridiculous, humiliating, monotonous.
>
> She was born Pamela Jean Byatt on 27 November 1920 in Ceylon,

---

Pamela Branch, *The Wooden Overcoat* (1951), *Lion in the Cellar* (1951),
Murder Every Monday (1954), and *Murder's Little Sister* (1958), are all in print
in paperback in the USA with Rue Morgue Press.

the daughter of a tea-planter. Her upbringing was that of a conventional colonial girl – or was it? Her earliest memory was of trying to persuade an elephant to swallow a home-made aspirin the size of a croquet ball. (The elephant did not oblige.) She claimed to have lived in Kashmir, learned Urdu, hunted with guns and with falcons, trained racehorses. The last at least seems unlikely; she later wrote, 'I hate and fear horses. There are a lot in the field next door. They watch me doing my face in the mornings. Our eyes *lock*. And it's perfectly apparent that they will never understand me and I never want to understand them at any price whatever.' What is certain is that she studied art in Paris after the Second World War, then came to London and attended RADA for a year. There she met Newton Branch, like her a bit of a fabulist, and married him. They went to live in Cyprus and both of them tried to write.

Pamela was more successful than her husband and sold her first novel to Robert Hale in 1949. Paper was rationed and books were still being produced to austere wartime standards. Before it appeared in print, she had finished her second and got herself a literary agent. She wrote to him on 7 June 1951:

> The contract for my first book, *The Wooden Overcoat*, was signed in October 1949. The book appeared in April 1951, the delay being attributed to an explosion. I have now had a letter from Mr Hale which tells me that the publication of my second book, *Lion in the Cellar*, has been postponed until 'early 1952'. The contract was signed in August 1950. I do appreciate the difficulties of the paper shortage, but surely this is an exaggeration? I do feel that at least there should have been a fire.

Her agent, David Higham, intervened and got publication brought forward to November 1951.

In *The Wooden Overcoat* Pamela Branch had brought a fresh new voice to crime writing. There had been humorous crime novels before, but none that poked such fun at murder. She was to continue in this vein for the rest of her short career. *The Wooden Overcoat* introduced its readers to the Asterisk Club, a residential establishment on the Embankment in Chelsea, whose membership is limited to wrongly acquitted murderers. The Club is run by Clifford Flush, once known as the Balliol Butcher, who since 1937 has lost no fewer than three women friends, all of whom have mysteriously fallen from moving trains. Flush, who now realizes it to be an unsatisfactory method unless put into operation over a viaduct, tells a prospective new member of the Club,

> The fourth survived. They brought her into Court in plaster of Paris . . . Of course, when I was acquitted, I was obliged to marry the woman. Mercifully it lasted a bare three months. She committed suicide. Don't look like that, old chap! I assure you I was in Aix les Bains at the time – which was perhaps fortuitous, because, as a final disagreeable gesture, she jumped off the Flying Scotsman.

The Asterisk Club's premises are a distinguished, ivy-clad eighteenth-century house. Its members include Mrs Barratt, who has lost more than one husband in questionable circumstances; Colonel Quincey, the treasurer, a man of few prepositions; Lily Cluj, a redhead with green eyes; and the Creaker, so called from the prolonged squeak on two descending notes made by his wooden leg. He had been tried and sentenced to death in 1937. 'His crime was . . . unattractive . . . However, owing to his comprehensive acquaintance with the underworld, he was able to produce certain spurious evidence which earned his reprieve.'

The Wooden Overcoat concerns a murder committed in the house next door to the Club. The neighbours' attempt to dispose of the body is inept. With some difficulty, they dump it over the parapet above the river, but they fail to notice that the tide is out. It is time for the Club to step in and sort out the amateurs. The results are wonderfully comic and, as in all good detective stories, it is not until the last page that the true murderer is exposed.

Pamela and Newton returned to London briefly before settling in Ireland where she wrote her second book, *Lion in the Cellar*. This is a perfect Ealing Comedy of a novel, in which Sukie Heap is in possession of an embarrassing corpse. She doesn't dare call in the police, as her family have all been in the business of murder and suspicion would surely fall upon her. She would have liked to consult Uncle George but 'decided immediately against it. He would be shocked to the core. He would probably hand her over to the police at once.' Unbeknownst to her, Uncle George is a successful serial killer whom the newspapers have dubbed The Strangler. So, although Sukie is innocent of the killing, she conceives an ingenious plan for disposal of the body which involves substituting it for a very large stuffed lion.

In her third novel, *Murder Every Monday* (1954), written in London and various rented cottages in England, Pamela returned to the Asterisk Club. Clifford Flush has not murdered anyone for years, but when he feels the urge to kill his bridge partner – the man's bidding is really quite unforgivable – he is blackmailed into leaving London. He and his fellow members set up a school in the ugliest manor-house in Dorset and conduct weekly residential courses. Flush teaches Grips, Knots, Electricity, Court Etiquette and Alibis. Mrs Barratt is in charge of Anatomy and Forensic Medicine, and Colonel Quincey specializes in Cars and Firearms. All goes well until a student is murdered on the premises.

Murder's Little Sister followed in 1958 and is as comic as her earlier novels, but it was the last to appear.

Pamela's marriage to Newton ended in 1960. Always broke, she worked that year as a Christmas postwoman. Two years earlier, she had written to her agent, 'I am trying to write a straight novel – a non-whodunit. I don't know whether this is a mistake, but I do feel I've more or less exhausted that other vein.' In 1962 her divorce finally became absolute, 'after which the whole world is – well, if not exactly my oyster – anyway my mussel'.

She was a glamorous woman, sophisticated, slim and elegant, with cupid-bow lips and masses of dark hair. 'Beautiful, marvellous Pamela, with eyelashes like bent hairpins', wrote Christianna Brand.

Shortly after her divorce, Pamela married Wing-Commander James Stuart-Lyon. 'I expect I shall get used to my resounding new name in time but at the moment I still can't say it without a small guffaw.' After trying unsuccessfully to find a Scottish fishing pub to buy, Pamela and James went off to live in Ghana where he served as air attaché at the High Commission. In 1963 she wrote, 'Out here, if anybody finds out that you write, you are immediately suspect. You at once get the However-do-you-*think*-of-it-all? treatment, then the Everybody-says-*I*-ought-to-write-a-book-I-write-such-descriptive-letters or the Honestly-my-life-would-make-a-marvellous-story (high-pitched giggle) . . .' She went on:

> My own little number progresses very, very slowly. It's almost impossible to work out here. The heat is stupefying and it's curiously difficult to concentrate. Then there are always people nipping and popping. 'No, no, I won't have a drink, I *know* you're working, I'm only going to stay for *five seconds.*' And two hours and four gins later, 'Oh, I am *awful!* But you've still got twenty minutes before dinner, haven't you?'

Pamela died of cancer in 1967 at the age of 47. There is no trace of the novel she was working on at the time, but she left behind four perfect gems of comic mystery. There have been other writers of funny detective fiction but none quite like her. Her quirky characters are entirely believable and her outlook, though odd, is always endearing. Reading her books makes one look differently at the world; nothing seems quite straightforward after you've finished one of them.

BRUCE HUNTER spent half a century as a literary agent at David Higham Associates.

How to Enjoy the Blackout

RUTH A. SYMES

My father used to say that one of the most dispiriting things about his childhood during the Second World War was the boredom. The very real fear of being bombed was one thing, but being cooped up in a blacked-out room or air-raid shelter with nothing to do was quite another. Certainly in the early 1940s families were thrown upon their own resources and their own company in a most unaccustomed way.

My father was saved from the tedium by the cheerful yellow-covered *Brighter Blackout Book*, published by George Allen & Unwin in 1939. This sturdy volume, laid out and illustrated to be easily read by torchlight, was written by the radio scriptwriter Howard Thomas (assisted by Marjorie Banks). Thomas had written many of the BBC's biggest radio shows, and was determined to create a book that would not only entertain but also meet the challenges of the times.

The *Brighter Blackout Book* did both these things. Though much of its content was based on Victorian parlour games that had been popular earlier in the century, a great deal of it had been tweaked to reflect the background of the war. Crossword puzzles, for example, were shaped like swastikas, and in the familiar 'inky blobs' game, participants were asked to use their pens to transform ink stains on paper into 'say – a portrait of Hitler, or a barrage balloon or Old Bill in his gas mask'. Readers were also challenged to complete a series of limericks which were nearly all, like this one, on war themes:

Howard Thomas and Marjorie A. Banks (eds.), *Brighter Blackout Book* (1939), is out of print.

There once was a warden of Slough,
Who got a black eye in a row,
He once met a WAAF out
In a terrible blackout

....

My father particularly enjoyed a game called Soap Boxes, in which players had to make two-minute speeches on topics chosen by other members of the family. As an extra challenge, the speeches had to be made in the style of someone famous – for example, 'Why I prefer pyjamas to night shirts' in the manner of Hitler or 'How I like my egg' in the style of Mussolini. Children playing the games in the *Brighter Blackout Book* would have been in no danger of forgetting that the country was at war, or who the enemy was.

The war spirit – active, participatory, competitive and above all British – imbues every page. In the Blackout Pronunciation Bee, players are encouraged to speak with Received Pronunciation: 'debris = day-bree; haricot = har-ee-ko; courteous = ker-tee-us'. The Blackout Spelling Bee, meanwhile, includes such abidingly difficult words as 'heinous' and 'spinach'.

The book contains many 'get-together' activities designed to encourage maximum family involvement, including the script of a play by Edgar Wallace entitled *The Forest of Happy Dreams* to be acted out. Readers are also urged to demonstrate bravery with the Blackout Nerve Test consisting of 'blood-curdling elements from the classics of fiction' – in other words, two short stories by Edgar Allan Poe, 'The Pit and the Pendulum' and 'Black Cat'. 'Read this with the lights turned off, except the lamp by which you read,' says the editor, 'but, if you're nervous, skip this and turn to the "Radio" section.'

At the start of the war, the world was growing wary, and children were encouraged to be alert. 'How to Avoid a Mental Blackout' includes puzzles to test intelligence, crosswords, chess problems, and guessing and word games. A section on the 'Black Arts' describes how to read people's characters and likely futures from their faces, dreams and palms. Handwriting is analysed as another guide to character, demonstrated by the signatures of such well-known people as the explorer Rosita Forbes and the singer Marie Burke.

For the later, more solitary hours of the evening there are short, thought-provoking pieces to read, including an extract from *I Married a German* by Madeleine Kent, and 'On Marriage' by Bertrand Russell. In a section on what the famous are reading, Forces' sweetheart Gracie Fields names *The Forsyte Saga* as her particular favourite, while the comedian Arthur Askey chooses *The Good Companions*. The Prime Minister's wife, Mrs Neville Chamberlain, has an entire half-page devoted to her choices, which include *The Wandering Scholars* by Helen Waddell and *Tales of a Grandfather* by Sir Walter Scott.

The *Brighter Blackout Book* must have lit up many a home and air-raid shelter in the dark wartime evenings. Its editor hoped that it had 'snatch reading appeal' – something between a quick read (a magazine or newspaper) and a full-length novel or political book. Certainly there can never have been a dull moment; the final sections are entitled 'Blackout Radio' (mock radio scripts), 'Blackout Singing' (a selection of sing-along sheet music) and 'Blackout Pastimes', in which readers are encouraged to make toys from household odds and ends such as wooden pegs and powder puffs.

Yet despite the book's up-beat tone, the seriousness of Britain's daily situation is never far from the surface. Some of the profits from sales of the *Brighter Blackout Book* were destined for the *Daily Sketch* War Relief Fund which, readers were assured, would provide soldiers, airmen and sailors with cigarettes, dart boards, dominoes, draughts, musical instruments, playing cards, boxing gloves and footballs.

As Thomas reminded his readers at the beginning of the book, *these* were the people who, after all, were really 'not having much fun'.

RUTH A. SYMES is a historian and freelance writer who lives in Manchester. She is rather relieved that she has never had to put the *Brighter Blackout Book* to use.

A Glorious Contradiction

JULIET GARDINER

Writing one's autobiography involves a certain audacity: the presumption that one has a story to tell, that one can tell it engagingly, that there will be publishers willing to publish, readers eager to read and, in the dark reaches of the night, benign reviewers. But a life told in *five* volumes when the subject is but 'nearing fifty and the grey hairs are beginning to show', and is generally regarded as a second-rate author? Step forward Sir Osbert Sitwell, to enthusiastic applause.

I came across Sitwell's autobiography years ago in a second-hand bookshop and I see that I paid £9.50 for all five volumes. I was attracted by the jackets, featuring baroque architectural details in rose and sepia that looked as if they had been drawn by John Piper, whose rather gothic pen-and-ink illustrations do indeed pepper the text, but were in fact the work of H. Crudwell.

I was also attracted by the endpapers of smudgy palm prints which echo the title of the first volume, *Left Hand, Right Hand*, and the theme of all five. Osbert was interested in chiromancy (and in the paranormal too) and was convinced of the palmists' belief that 'the lines of the left hand are incised unalterably at birth, while those of the right hand are modified by our actions, environment and the life we lead'. Having read only one of Osbert's novels, *Before the Bombardment* (1926), generally regarded as his best, and having just finished Victoria Glendinning's scintillating but sad biography

---

Osbert Sitwell, *Left Hand, Right Hand* (1945), *The Scarlet Tree* (1946), *Great Morning* (1948), *Laughter in the Next Room* (1949), and *Noble Essences* (1950), are out of print.

of Osbert's poet sister Edith, I was ripe for the experience of his memoirs – memoirs that proved a phenomenal publishing success, particularly in America where they found an audience avid to have their view of the eccentricities of the English aristocracy confirmed.

I read the five volumes – a total of 1,500 pages – with rising, then falling, then reviving enchantment. If time is short, however, I'd advise reading *Left Hand, Right Hand* and the fourth volume, *Laughter in the Next Room*, missing out the intervening two and the final volume (*Noble Essences*, a series of essays about writers and artists Osbert knew – 'great fellow egoists', as V. S. Pritchett characterized them).

The first four volumes are largely sequential – though there is a lot of revisiting and serpentine diversions and digressions within each – and follow Osbert's passage through life, with long asides on his semi-distinguished forebears. He notes of the Second World War, the period in which he was writing these volumes, that 'there are no signposts to tell you where you are': there are not many in his memoirs either. *Laughter in the Next Room* ends in 1948 with Sitwell, 'an Englishman who saw the world's greatest darkness gathering . . . strain[ing] toward the dawn of a new age', having evoked in loving detail 'what it was like to be alive before the world fell into the pit'.

Francis Osbert Sacheverell Sitwell (he succeeded to the baronetcy when his father died in 1943) was born on 6 December 1892 in a house that backed on to the Ritz Hotel, into a family that was wealthy on both sides and very grand through the maternal line. His mother, Ida, was the beautiful, if not over-bright, daughter of the first Earl of Londesborough; his father was Sir George Reresby Sitwell, a genealogist and antiquary and a very odd fish indeed. Edith was five years older than he; his brother Sacheverell, five years younger.

Osbert was very proud of his lineage which he liked to think could be traced back in a direct line to the Plantagenets (though his friend Evelyn Waugh once pointed out that an awful lot of people could do that too if they were prepared to put in the hours). He was also close to his siblings (until Sacheverell married out and a chill entered the relationship): indeed the three formed almost a corporation since all became aesthetes, poets and writers, with varying degrees of success. Their most famous outing was their joint performance of *Façade*, in which the troika experimented with speaking words to the rhythm of dance measures while Edith recited poems through a sort of megaphone from behind a painted curtain with a hole cut in it, accompanied by music composed by William Walton.

This occasioned much fluttering when it was first performed in Lady Colefax's drawing-room in 1922, and derision at its first public performance the following year. (Noël Coward wrote a revue sketch about the Sitwells, whom he named the Whittlebots, which offended them greatly.) Osbert devotes an entire chapter in *Laughter in the Next Room* to the product-ion and evolution of *Façade* and notes that when it was performed twenty years later, during the Blitz, even the firemen were enthusiastic.

Osbert, Edith and Sacheverell

Though the Sitwells had been landowners for 700 years, the family coffers had been hugely swelled by in-dustry. In the seventeenth century they built an iron works which became the world's pre-eminent manufacturer of nails, enabling the building of the family seat, Renishaw Hall in Derbyshire. More than 200 years later Osbert's grandmother exploited the discovery of a rich seam of coal in the grounds, and his father cannily invested in South African mining shares – which was just as well. The Sitwells were profligate – one might say incontinent – spenders, stuffing Renishaw, their houses in Scarborough and London, and a crumbling palazzo in Italy with fine furniture, paintings, sculpture and valuable *objets*.

The garden at Renishaw was a particular delight to Osbert: indeed he opens his memoir with a eulogy to its architecture

> of green walls and box . . . the formal arrangement of beds and
> statues and yew hedges beyond [which] lies the Wilderness,
> part of a wild garden surviving from the 18th century, with
> dark, mysterious cut glades . . . here in the spring, when the
> trees are burgeoning, the ground is covered for three weeks at a
> time with the azure snow of bluebells and later, in the summer,
> you find the tall, overweighted spires of wild Canterbury bells,
> no doubt descended from flowers escaped long ago from older
> enclosed gardens of monasteries and manors.

We first meet Osbert's father in the gardens that both fulfill and
characterize him in his son's mind, a man for whom 'the Middle Ages
are a model for all life to follow'.

> All day long he can be found . . . surveying his work which will
> never be finished, his head full of new projects of sun and
> shade, but never of flowers, measuring the various views with a
> stick to his eye or a pair of binoculars. Sometimes he is plan-
> ning a boat of stone upon the lake, or a dragon in lead,
> writhing for a quarter of a mile through its level waters, or a
> colonnaded pavilion upon another island, or a Roman aque-
> duct in counterfeit to frame the prospect with its elongated
> arches, or a cascade to fall down a stone channel for a hundred
> and fifty feet, from the water to the garden below: and, for proj-
> ects such as these, though most of them never materialized, he
> would cause wooden towers, built up of planks and joists and
> beams – like an early machine for siege warfare or a drawing by
> Piranesi – to be erected here and there at the right points of
> vantage.

Osbert was sent away from Renishaw to Eton, which he liked
'except . . . for work, and games, boys and masters'. He then joined

the Hussars but was miserable since he claimed to prefer giraffes to horses. So, as he describes in *Great Morning*, he transferred to the Grenadier Guards, where his obligations seem to have comprised a few hours' duty at the Tower of London, which allowed him plenty of time to indulge his interest in the theatre, music and art.

On the outbreak of the First World War, Osbert was sent to the Front and he took part as a temporary captain in the battle of Loos. But soon a poisoned finger served as a Blighty and he was back in London, where he became a feature on the metropolitan scene. Osbert simply knew 'everyone' – Evelyn Waugh, Gertrude Stein, Arnold Bennett, Aldous Huxley, T. S. Eliot. He made illustrious enemies too, including Winston Churchill and the Leavises.

Osbert Sitwell was, it must be said, a snob – he had absolutely no interest in the middle classes whom he seemed to think intervened in the natural order of things, coming between the landed classes and their servants. He was an anti-Semite. He could be malicious. And, as is often the case with waspish souls, he took offence easily. He was particularly scornful of his father, who, admittedly, was easy to ridicule, with his inventions of a singing toothbrush and an 'egg' for use in polar regions or the desert. This latter consisted of meat surrounded by rice, encased in lime, a wheeze that, at the suggestion of the mischievous Osbert, he took straight to Gordon Selfridge, who showed him the door. But his father was in fact no fool, probably cleverer than Osbert and certainly nicer, and the amount of space Sir George takes up in his son's autobiographies (which were not published until after his father's death) suggests how profoundly enmeshing their relationship was.

In parts the memoirs sing with vitality, enthusiasm, prolix detail and wonderfully telling observations. On the whole they skate over life's little difficulties, including Osbert's relationship with his even more snobbish long-term companion and lover David Horner. In other parts the prose becomes clotted, excessive and self-regarding. If Vita Sackville-West wrote with a brass nib, as Virginia Woolf observed, it could be said that Osbert sometimes dipped his in violet-scented honey. Even so, the books are peerless as a portrait of a very strange English family, epitomized in John Singer Sargent's group portrait commissioned by Sir George in 1900.

Sargent was apparently chosen because Sir George had heard that he was the best, and he packed up furniture from Renishaw to transport to London for the sittings – though he forgot to include any ornaments and had to borrow a selection from the wealthy connoisseur Sir Joseph Duveen. Sir George himself posed in brown leather riding boots (though he never rode), his hand resting on Edith's shoulder like a puppet master. (Sargent declined to redesign the maligned aquiline nose of Edith.) Lady Ida wore a large hat with a ball gown and was portrayed arranging flowers (which of course she never did at home, given the retinue of servants), while Osbert and Sachie can be seen in the corner feeding a biscuit to their pug. Each member of the family stares straight out of the canvas, remote from one another.

However, Osbert's memoirs reflect more than his strange family life. He was never in any doubt as to his relevance to the world, and his engagement with it was in every sense unconventional. He took the General Strike in 1926 very hard – 'never have I been more disturbed, save by the two declarations of World War'. He sympathized with the plight of the miners because he'd seen their hard and hazardous lives in his own family's mines (though a visitor to Renishaw, catching sight of a black-faced gang coming off shift, mistook them for chimney sweeps). So when the strike started he declined to join his upper-class mates in their 'holiday romp' of driving buses or working on the railways, and instead sat, as he put it in *Laughter in the Next Room*, 'the very picture of a drone in an armchair [in his house in Chelsea] . . . in a room full of complicated and brittle decoration . . . wondering what could be done'.

Eventually, invited to suggest 'a cry suitable for the hoardings in this emergency' since he was reckoned to be good with words, Osbert came up with the puzzlingly enigmatic slogan – 'Think Less and Eat More', which he subsequently changed to 'Eat Less and Think More' (unsurprisingly neither appears to have been adopted). He also decided to use his influence via a lunch with Lady Wimborne – since 'we were distantly related' through the Duke of Wellington. As the taxicabs were on strike, Osbert had to walk from Chelsea to Piccadilly where, revived by a dry Martini, he urged Alice Wimborne to encourage her husband to invite the trades union leaders to Wimborne House to effect a settlement. It turned out that Lord Wimborne had already put this in train. Yet Osbert returned home well satisfied that he had played a part in 'introducing a true vision' of reconciliation.

If all this sounds like society tittle-tattle about serious matters, in a way it is, but it does give one an intimate glimpse of the workings of a section of English society now long gone. Osbert's inconsequential observations – bananas, for example, were regarded as very 'common' fruit, not to be consumed in the Sitwell nursery – are intermingled with idiosyncratic asides about his own circle, and public figures of the day. These include the observation that, as a freshwater fisherman, Chamberlain was not the best person to be in charge of the nation's foreign policy when war threatened – 'I doubt if Lord Palmerston was a fisherman.'

One of the last generation to be brought up by candlelight, Osbert Sitwell was a glorious contradiction: a moderate voice among the philistine and the bellicose, an aristocratic snob for whom the artist was the only true superior being, a rococo figure who energetically promoted modernism, a promising meteor that all too quickly fizzled out.

JULIET GARDINER's last book was about the 1930s and she now very much wants to know more about the preceding decades – and write about them.

Summer Sunrise, Winter Twilight

ANTHONY LONGDEN

Numbed with despair over the threat to the fragile beauty of the Chilterns and the villages of Buckinghamshire posed by the new high-speed rail link, I went in search of solace. I badly needed a dose of that reassuring country writing which once enjoyed such a boom, but which now seems to have slipped out of fashion. For me, the first and only choice was J. H. B. Peel.

Thirty or so years ago, John Hugh Brignal Peel would have needed no introduction. For years he wrote a fortnightly column, 'Country Talk', for the *Daily Telegraph*, essays subsequently gathered into a series of books; he was a talented poet; and in later years he appeared regularly on country-themed television and radio programmes.

His style is neither that of a nature notebook nor the ramblings of a rural weekender. Rather, he revived the art of the essay and in doing so provided a true picture of what country life really means in our time, not only its surface but also its deep-rooted patterns and perennial challenges. He writes of farming and hunting; of shepherds and postmen and squires; of ancient monuments, historic buildings, modern motorways. Above all, he tells us of the things that rarely make news – summer sunrise, winter twilight, the look of the land. This is the pulse of rural Britain, recorded by a poet of whom John Masefield said: 'Mr Peel knows more than any other living man about the life of the English countryside.'

J. H. B. Peel, *The Chilterns* (1950), *Portrait of Exmoor* (1970), *Country Talk* (1970), *Light and Shade* (1976), and *Country Talk Continued* (1979), are all out of print.

J. H. B. Peel spent a third of his life living high in a remote part of the Chilterns and then moved to an even lonelier part of Exmoor, writing extensively about both, but he also travelled around 20,000 miles a year throughout Britain gathering material for his work. An early example of his flair for description came in his book *The Chilterns* (1950), published as part of the publisher Paul Elek's 'Visions of England' series.

> In the valley, yet so deeply set that you cannot see them, lie a farmhouse, two flint cottages, and a barn whose switch-back roof is encrusted with the moss and lichen and green-gold rind that need a century in which to season, and two centuries in which to mature. Smoke from the farm sidles up – blue and veerless and lazy – but its source, the chimneys, is invisible, hidden by the brow's sheer slope.
>
> Ahead, and perhaps one mile away, the valley's opposite flank climbs to meet the skyline, stretching to left and right as far as the eye can see, and all the way plumed by beechwoods that are sombre in winter, gaudy in autumn, sedate in summer, and in spring a vast nave of fluted and delicate emerald . . .

Peel was born in 1913, and came from an old North Devon family. He went to Merchant Taylors' School in Northwood, Middlesex, and then up to Oriel College, Oxford. During the Second World War he served as a naval officer, and he remained a keen sailor for the rest of his life. Indeed, several of his essays combine his two loves – of land and sea. Here, for example, is his arrival in a quiet tributary of the Helford River in Cornwall at dusk:

> When I went below, the clock said midnight or Middle Watch; the barometer was poised between Fair and Very Dry; the dog slept on his locker seat. Utter peace prevailed, the only man-made sound being a simmer from the stove. And there I sat, in a glow of gentle light in a world of creaking sibilance, less than

two miles from telephones and transistors, yet feeling as though I were a day's voyage from the nearest inhabited island.

He would doubtless have been appalled, though probably not surprised, by the advent of the high-speed rail plan. In *Country Talk*, back in 1970, he described what he saw as the fatal decline of Great Missenden in Buckinghamshire: 'During the 1950s, however, the village began to show disturbing symptoms. Commercial travellers took to using the street as a short cut, which meant that the street became a main road. More commuters arrived, bristling the station with briefcases. Meadows fetched many pieces of silver, not because the natives needed houses, but because the strangers demanded dormitories.'

In Peel's view, suburbs were all very well, but they spelled death for places like Great Missenden. 'Anyone who pretends otherwise is equating "life" with shops, season tickets, and estate agents.' Though this essay was written more than forty years ago, Peel had already spotted a pattern of decline with which we are now all too familiar.

I have the suburbanite's classic love of the countryside and its people, and have fed it with the likes of George Ewart Evans, H. J. Massingham, Cecil Torr, Richard Mabey, Alison Uttley, Roger Deakin and S. L. Bensusan. But somehow J. H. B. Peel is in an entirely different league. His portraits of characters are moving and poetical, and there is always the strong sense of genuine emotion. A regular theme throughout his *County Talk* series was visits to a man he described as 'the Chiltern hermit', who lived alone in a remote cottage 'atop a steep hill' – in much the same way as Peel did himself.

In one tale, Peel relates the local vicar's concern when he hears the hermit has not been seen for some time. The man is eventually traced to a nearby hospital. The vicar sets off to visit him and is surprised to find such a rustic and apparently poor countryman in a private room. The hermit is quick to explain: 'Oi value my privacy. Oi always 'ave done, ever since my auntie took to growing roses round the garden toilet. "One o' these days," oi said to myself, "you're going to need a hoperation, and you won't loike it when they take your teeth out in front of all them other patients. So", oi said, "you'd better do something about it.'" He had 'put summat by' each month, and was pleased with the result.

Peel can have a persuasive effect on his readers, too, as I found when his knowledgeable writing compelled me to buy a walking-stick, my trusty companion still, twenty years later (silver birch and bought in Chagford, by the way). He owned several sticks, matching each to the terrain or occasion.

> Myself, I prefer ash, a light yet strong companion. In youth it wears a grey bloom; in age, a subdued gloss, deepened by mud and some honourable scars. Beware the stick with a curved handle, for the curve was imposed artificially, and will begin to uncurl after a few months. Handles should form a right angle with the rest of the stick, and the angle itself should result from natural growth. On short walks there is much to be said for sticks with a knobbly handle, about the size of a pullet's egg, which fits like a castor in the palm of the hand.
>
> At the other extreme comes the blackthorn, a self-defensive companion, much favoured in the years when criminals carried cudgels. My own blackthorn weighs nearly three pounds, and could crack the thickest skull. It is indeed a stick, descended etymologically from the Old Teutonic *stik*, meaning 'to pierce'.

Despite his prodigious output, Peel remains something of an enigma. He was clearly a confirmed loner by nature his one attempt at marriage did not last – and he certainly did not care for London. One of his essays in *Country Talk Again* sums it up neatly: 'London and I get along very well without each other.' But he was very fond of dogs and one in particular, Shap, a Lakeland Terrier, became a familiar sight by his side on television.

This close bond brought out some of the very best of Peel's writing, and his description of Shap's declining years still brings a tear to my eye.

In his thirteenth year Shap walked twenty miles between dawn and dusk and then asked for an after-dinner stroll. In his fourteenth year, however, his sight and hearing lost something of their keenness . . . In his sixteenth year, he could still plod a mile uphill. Indeed, I had sometimes to restrain his doggedness lest he should strain his heart.

Last night he complained of not feeling well, and a few hours later he died, swiftly and easily, with his head in my hands. Such is the price of love, which exacts nothing less than a part of ourselves, great or small, according as the occasion and our temperament decree. A dog is, of course, only a dog. His death is universal and not new. Two thousand years ago a Greek countryman suffered a similar bereavement, whereof the monument was discovered by archaeologists. 'If', said the inscription, 'you pass this way, and happen to notice this stone, do not laugh, even although it is only a dog's grave. Tears fell for my sake, and the earth was heaped above me by a master's hand, who likewise carved these words.'

J. H. B. Peel died where he had lived, in a tiny two-bedroom cottage in Charles parish on Exmoor, in 1983. A year later, the *Daily Telegraph* paid for a fittingly practical monument to him – a toposcope at County Gate nearby, which describes the panorama over the East Lyn and Badgworthy valleys.

ANTHONY LONGDEN spent 30 years in local newspapers around London and sat on the Press Complaints Commission until its recent demise. Now a consultant, he can frequently be found wedged into the narrower reaches of the Topography stacks at the London Library, indulging his passion for country writing.

Flouting Destiny

ROGER JONES

British publishers, we're told, turn out around 200,000 new titles every year. That is not a trivial number. In fact, it's so large a number that one can't really think any useful thoughts about it. Even if cut down to manageable size by the ruthless application of Sturgeon's Law ('Ninety per cent of everything is garbage'), the mind still flounders.

Under these circumstances, it behoves anyone sitting down to write a book and add one more to the print mountain, to ask themselves the careful and sober question, 'Why am I doing this?'

'No man but a blockhead ever wrote, except for money,' said Dr Johnson. This will be a sufficient answer for some, but it can hardly be said to have settled the question once and for all. However much one admires Johnson's rocklike common sense, it has to be admitted that it was allied to some fairly rocklike prejudices. In fact there are at least five other possible reasons for writing.

First there is Orwell's suggestion – REVENGE! Which in turn is a special case of a more general phenomenon – the writer's desire to order reality into a more satisfactory form than that in which he has actually experienced it. Second is the desire to change the world, to mould reality by moulding men's thoughts. Third is the desire simply to arrange one's own thoughts. Fourth is vanity (which doesn't exclude other motives). And fifth is what we might call the Ancient Mariner scenario – the urge to tell someone something.

My vote is for the last of these. The way I see it is this: because we can only apprehend the world through our senses, we tend to think of it as something outside ourselves. But it may well be that the shoe is actually on the other foot: it is not external to us; we are external to it. Reality is a walled and secret garden and we are on the outside, trying to see in. We peep through holes and cracks, we dangle precariously from branches of overhanging trees, we balance on wobbly ladders, we stand on each others' shoulders, we squint from strange angles, we devise periscopes and spyglasses.

Our reward is snatched and fuzzy glimpses, no two the same, no one complete. So, trying always to construct a larger picture of the world, we compare notes. That is why people talk to each other. And that is why people write books. And why other people read them. Writing, quite simply, is the continuation of talking by other means. 'Communication is life,' said Virginia Woolf.

Helen Waddell in her *Mediaeval Latin Lyrics* (1929) quotes some lines of the ninth-century theologian Hrabanus Maurus, Archbishop of Mainz, and provides a beautiful translation:

> No work of men's hands, but the weary years
> besiege and take it; comes its evil day.
> The written word alone flouts destiny,
> revives the past, and gives the lie to death.

I like to think that future generations will turn not to our computer hard-drives but to our books when they ask themselves what kind of people we were.

ROGER JONES is a part-time shop-assistant living in Hampshire. His most recent publication, co-written with Mike Ware, is *What's Who? A dictionary of things named after people and the people they are named after.*

94

Bibliography

H. E. Bates, *The Darling Buds of May* 24

The *Book of Common Prayer* (1662) 57

Pamela Branch, *The Wooden Overcoat*; *Lion in the Cellar*; *Murder Every Monday*; *Murder's Little Sister* 73

Pamela Brown, *The Swish of the Curtain* 42

A. C. Burnell and Henry Yule, *Hobson-Jobson, A Glossary of Colloquial Anglo-Indian Words and Phrases* 63

Denis Constanduros, *My Grandfather* & *Father, Dear Father* 12

Ulysses S. Grant, *Personal Memoirs* 46

A. R. B. Haldane, *The Drove Roads of Scotland* 18

Nigel B. Hankin, *Hanklyn-Janklin or A Stranger's Rumble-Tumble Guide to Some Words, Customs and Quiddities Indian and Indo-British* 63

Rachel Khoo, *The Little Paris Kitchen* 7

D. H. Lawrence, *Lady Chatterley's Lover* 52

Mollie Panter-Downes, *At the Pines* 29

J. H. B. Peel, *The Chilterns*; *Portrait of Exmoor*; *Country Talk*; *Light and Shade*; *Country Talk Continued* 88

Osbert Sitwell, *Left Hand, Right Hand*; *The Scarlet Tree*; *Great Morning*; *Laughter in the Next Room*; *Noble Essences* 81

Howard Thomas and Marjorie A. Banks (eds.), *Brighter Blackout Book* 78

Evelyn Waugh, The *Sword of Honour* trilogy: *Men at Arms, Officers and Gentlemen, Unconditional Surrender* 34

Coming attractions . . .

DERVLA MURPHY sails to the Cape

CHARLES ELLIOTT salutes a woman warrior

ALLISON PEARSON meets Mrs Miniver

DENNIS BUTTS writes to Major Westerman

CAROLINE CHAPMAN reads Sybille Bedford

GORDON BOWKER turns ultramarine

CATHERINE MERRICK discovers biophilia